Excel

Moira Stephen

TEACH YOURSELF BOOKS

Orders: please contact Bookpoint Ltd, 39 Milton Park, Abingdon, Oxon OX14 4TD. Telephone: (44) 01235 400414, Fax: (44) 01235 400454. Lines are open from 9.00 – 6.00, Monday to Saturday, with a 24 hour message answering service. Email address: orders@bookpoint.co.uk

Long-renowned as the authoritative source for self-guided learning – with more than 30 million copies sold worldwide – the *Teach Yourself* series includes over 200 titles in the fields of languages, crafts, hobbies, business and education.

British Library Cataloguing in Publication Data
A catalogue record for this title is available from The British Library

ISBN 0 340 70491 8

First published 1998
Impression number   10 9 8 7 6 5 4 3 2
Year   2004 2003 2002 2001 2000 1999 1998

The 'Teach Yourself' name and logo are registered trade marks of Hodder & Stoughton Ltd.

Copyright © 1998 Moira Stephen

All rights reserved. No part of this publication may be reproduced or transmitted in any form or by any means, electronic or mechanical, including photocopy, recording, or any information storage and retrieval system, without permission in writing from the publisher or under licence from the Copyright Licensing Agency Limited. Further details of such licences (for reprographic reproduction) may be obtained from the Copyright Licensing Agency Limited, of 90 Tottenham Court Road, London W1P 9HE.

Typeset by MacDesign, Southampton
Printed in Great Britain for Hodder & Stoughton Educational,
a division of Hodder Headline Plc, 338 Euston Road, London NW1 3BH
by Cox & Wyman Ltd, Reading, Berkshire.

CONTENTS

1	**Getting started**	**1**
1.1	Aims of this chapter	1
1.2	Introducing Excel 97	1
1.3	Hardware and software	2
1.4	Installing Excel 97	3
1.5	Starting Excel 97	4
1.6	The Excel screen	6
1.7	Workbooks and worksheets	7
1.8	Menus	7
1.9	Help!	8
1.10	Exiting Excel 97	16
1.11	Summary	16
2	**Basic Excel skills**	**17**
2.1	Aims of this chapter	17
2.2	Spreadsheet jargon	17
2.3	Moving around your worksheet	19
2.4	Selection techniques	21
2.5	Entering text and data	23
2.6	Editing text and data	24
2.7	Column width	26
2.8	Text wrap within a cell	28
2.9	Number formats	30
2.10	Formulas	31
2.11	AutoFill	34
2.12	Another worksheet!	36
2.13	Moving or copying cells	37
2.14	Adjusting rows and columns	39
2.15	Save Workbook	39
2.16	Print Preview and Print	42
2.17	Close, Open and New	44
2.18	Summary	45

3 Formatting and layout — 46
3.1 Aims of this chapter — 46
3.2 Bold, italic and underline — 46
3.3 Alignment — 47
3.4 More formatting options — 49
3.5 Format Painter — 52
3.6 Change the default font — 53
3.7 Freeze panes — 54
3.8 Split screen — 55
3.9 Page layout — 56
3.10 Summary — 61

4 Working with sheets — 62
4.1 Aims of this chapter — 62
4.2 Moving between worksheets — 62
4.3 Worksheet design — 63
4.4 Adding worksheets — 64
4.5 Deleting worksheets — 66
4.6 Renaming worksheets — 67
4.7 Moving and copying worksheets — 67
4.8 Grouping worksheets — 68
4.9 Summary — 69

5 Formulas and functions — 70
5.1 Aims of this chapter — 70
5.2 AutoSum — 70
5.3 Formula Palette — 73
5.4 Statistical functions — 74
5.5 View formula — 77
5.6 Relative and absolute addresses — 79
5.7 Circular References — 82
5.8 Named ranges — 84
5.9 IF function — 90
5.10 Comments — 95
5.11 Cell protection — 97
5.12 Summary — 98

6 Charting and drawing — 99
6.1 Aims of this chapter — 99

6.2	Preparing your data	99
6.3	Chart Wizard	100
6.4	A chart in your worksheet	103
6.5	A chart on a separate sheet	106
6.6	Charts without the Wizard	106
6.7	Printing your chart	107
6.8	Default chart	108
6.9	Drawing tools	108
6.10	Some more options	111
6.11	Summary	113

7 AutoFormat, styles and templates — 114

7.1	Aims of this chapter	114
7.2	AutoFormat	114
7.3	Introducing styles	115
7.4	Working with styles	116
7.5	Workbook templates	118
7.6	Worksheet templates	120
7.7	Summary	122

8 Database features — 123

8.1	Aims of this chapter	123
8.2	Database terminology	123
8.3	Sort	124
8.4	AutoFilter	128
8.5	Advanced Filter	130
8.6	Data validation	133
8.7	Data Form	135
8.8	Summary	136

9 Macros — 137

9.1	Aims of this chapter	137
9.2	What are macros?	137
9.3	Recording your macro	138
9.4	Playing back your macro	140
9.5	Ideas for more macros	141
9.6	Deleting a macro	143
9.7	Editing a macro	144
9.8	Saving macros on exit	146
9.9	Summary	146

10 Toolbars — 147
- 10.1 Aims of this chapter — 147
- 10.2 Moving toolbars — 147
- 10.3 Showing and hiding toolbars — 148
- 10.4 Editing existing toolbars — 149
- 10.5 Creating a new toolbar — 152
- 10.6 Adding macros to toolbars — 152
- 10.7 Change the button image — 153
- 10.8 Assign a macro to a tool — 154
- 10.9 Resetting toolbars — 154
- 10.10 Summary — 156

11 Excel with other applications — 157
- 11.1 Aims of this chapter — 157
- 11.2 Linking vs embedding — 157
- 11.3 Copy and Paste — 158
- 11.4 Copy and Paste Special — 159
- 11.5 Insert Excel Worksheet — 160
- 11.7 Microsoft Map — 161
- 11.8 Summary — 168

12 Excel and the Web — 169
- 12.1 Aims of this chapter — 169
- 12.2 E-mail — 169
- 12.3 Hyperlinks — 173
- 12.4 Preparing a Web page — 176
- 12.5 Previewing your Web page — 178
- 12.6 Publishing to the Web — 179
- 12.7 Summary — 179

Index — 181

PREFACE

This book is aimed at the user who wants to use Excel 97 without having to become a computing or mathematical wizard! It doesn't matter if you're new to spreadsheets, or are familiar with spreadsheets but new to Excel 97, *Teach Yourself Excel 97* will have you up and running quickly and painlessly! It adopts a tutorial approach, providing examples of worksheets for you to set up and experiment with. I suggest you work through the chapters in the book in order, as each new chapter builds on the knowledge gained in the previous ones. This book discusses:

- Spreadsheet jargon and concepts, explained in layman's terms. You won't be bombarded with computer-speak!!
- Essential spreadsheet skills. Entering and editing text, data, formulas and functions are all explored.
- Formatting and layout. Effective presentation is essential if your data is to be easily understood by those who read it. Excel's formatting options will help you to achieve a professional finish.
- Charting and drawing. Pictures often speak louder than words! The charting and drawing options will add impact to your data.
- Automation. Find out how AutoFormat, templates, styles and macros can help you become more efficent.
- Database features. Do you need to sort lists of items, or find entries in your data? Excel's database features will help.
- Excel and the wider world. Powerful as Excel is, it can't do everything on its own! To help you achieve all that you require, you'll find that Excel works well with the other packages in Microsoft Office, and with the wider world through the Internet and World Wide Web!

You can use this book on your own, but it could also be used in the classroom, as it contains excercises and instructions.

I hope you enjoy using Teach Yourself Excel 97 – and have success with your spreadsheets.

Moira Stephen
November 1997

1

GETTING STARTED

1.1 Aims of this chapter

This chapter introduces the spreadsheet package Excel 97. We will start with an overview of the package, and consider the hardware and software specifications required to run Excel 97 successfully. We then move on to look at how you install the package on your computer. Getting into Excel 97, the working environment, on-line Help system and exiting Excel 97 will also be discussed.

1.2 Introducing Excel 97

Excel 97 is a very powerful spreadsheet package – but don't let that put you off! You can use Excel to produce simple spreadsheets to help you prepare your invoices, budgets and summary statements. You can also use Excel to chart your data, manipulate it using database-type features and publish your worksheet to the Web. Excel integrates well with the other packages in Microsoft Office 97 and you'll find out how you can use this to your advantage.

Finally, Excel 97 is very Web oriented – you'll soon be able to hyperlink to other files and Internet addresses, send e-mails and publish your worksheets and charts on the Web!

1.3 Hardware and software

To run Excel 97 successfully on your computer, it should meet the following minimum hardware and software specifications. The first set gives the system requirements for Excel 97 only, the second set gives details of additional requirements should you be installing the entire Microsoft Office 97 suite.

SPECIFICATION FOR EXCEL 97

Processor	486 or higher
Operating system	Windows 95 or Windows NT Workstation version 3.51 Service Pack 5 or later *NB. Excel 97 will not run on machines using earlier versions of Windows*
RAM	The more the better! At least 8 Mb with Windows 95; 16 Mb with Windows NT
Hard disk	Between 22 Mb and 64 Mb. A typical installation requires 36 Mb
CD-ROM drive	The package normally comes on CD (you have to specifically ask for the diskette version if you want it). The CD version is quicker to install and contains additional components, e.g. Microsoft Internet Explorer, extra Clip Art, video files and sound files
Disk drive	One 3.5" High Density disk drive (if you've bought the diskette version)
Monitor	VGA or higher resolution video adapter (SVGA 256 colour recommended)

Mouse   Microsoft mouse or compatible pointing device

Printer   Any Windows compatible printer

SPECIFICATION FOR MICROSOFT OFFICE 97

If you are installing the whole of the Microsoft Office 97 suite, the above specification applies, with the following amendments.

RAM   As above, but to be able to run 2 or more programs simultaneously, you'll definitely need more RAM.

Hard disk *Small Business Edition:*
A typical installation requires about 196 Mb

Standard Edition:
Between 60 Mb and 167 Mb. A typical installation requires about 102 Mb.

Professional Edition:
Between 73 Mb and 191 Mb. A typical installation requires approximately 121 Mb.

1.4 Installing Excel 97

If you have bought a new computer at the same time as the software, the software is most probably pre-installed on your hard disk. If this is the case you can skip this bit.

As the general trend is towards buying Office Suites (rather than individual applications) you have probably purchased Microsoft Office 97 in one of the three editions available:

- **Small Business Edition** with Excel, Word, Publisher and Outlook.

- **Standard Edition** with Excel, Word, PowerPoint and Outlook.

- **Professional Edition** with Excel, Word, PowerPoint, Outlook and Access.

EXCEL 97

The instructions below are for installing Microsoft Office 97 under Windows 95 – if you've bought Excel 97 on its own, follow the instructions included with your CD or disk set.

1 If you're installing from a CD, insert the Office CD in the CD-ROM drive on your computer

   If you're installing from floppy disks, insert the first Setup disk (Disk 1) in drive A or B

2 Click the **Start** button on the **Taskbar**

3 Choose **Settings**

4 Click **Control Panel**

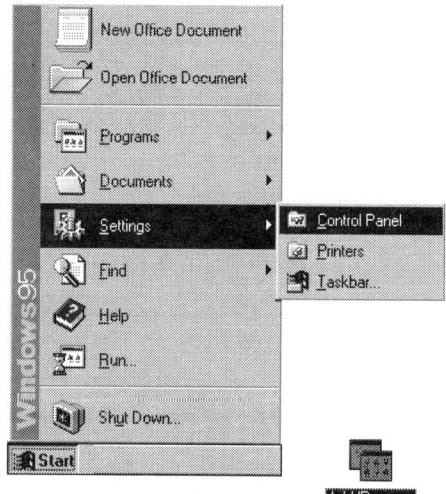

5 Double-click the **Add/Remove Programs** icon

6 On the **Install/Uninstall** tab, click the [Install...] button

7 Follow the Setup instructions on the screen

1.5 Starting Excel 97

Starting Excel 97 is very similar to starting any other Windows 95 application. You have 2 options available – the Start menu and the Shortcut Bar.

GETTING STARTED

THE START MENU

1. Click the **Start** button on the **Taskbar**
2. Choose **Programs**
3. Click **Microsoft Excel**

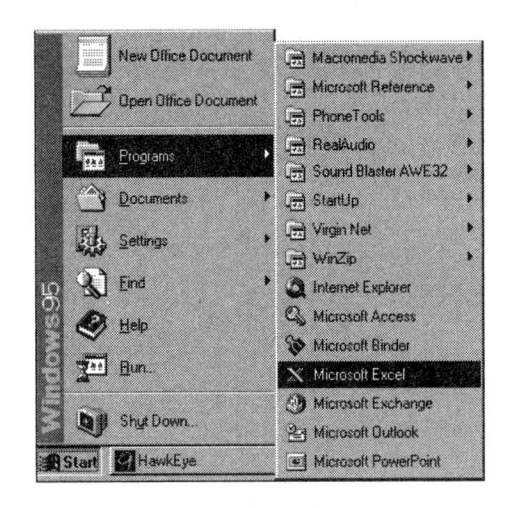

THE SHORTCUT BAR

1. If the **Microsoft Excel** tool is there, just click it!

Or

2. Click the **Start a new document** tool on the Shortcut Bar
3. At the **New Office Document** dialog box open the **General** tab

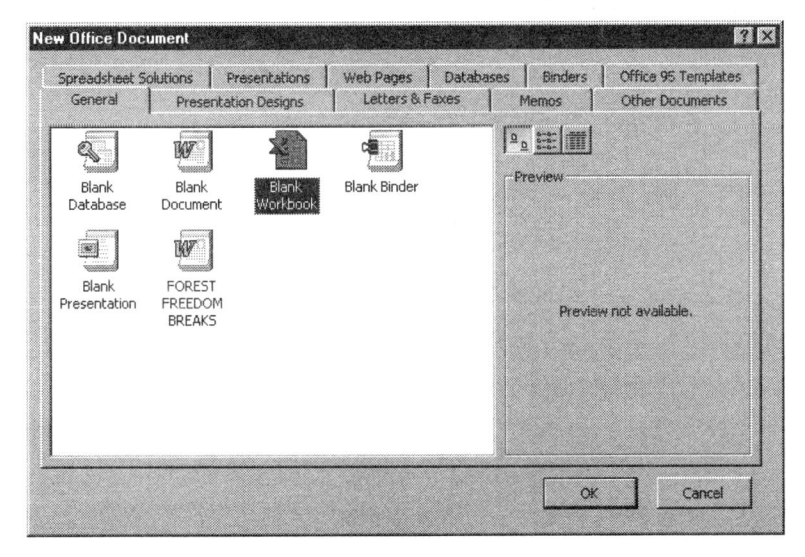

4 Select **Blank Workbook**
5 Click **OK**

1.6 The Excel screen

Whichever method you choose to start Excel, you are presented with a new workbook displaying a blank worksheet. We'll take a tour of the Excel screen, so that you know what the various areas are called.

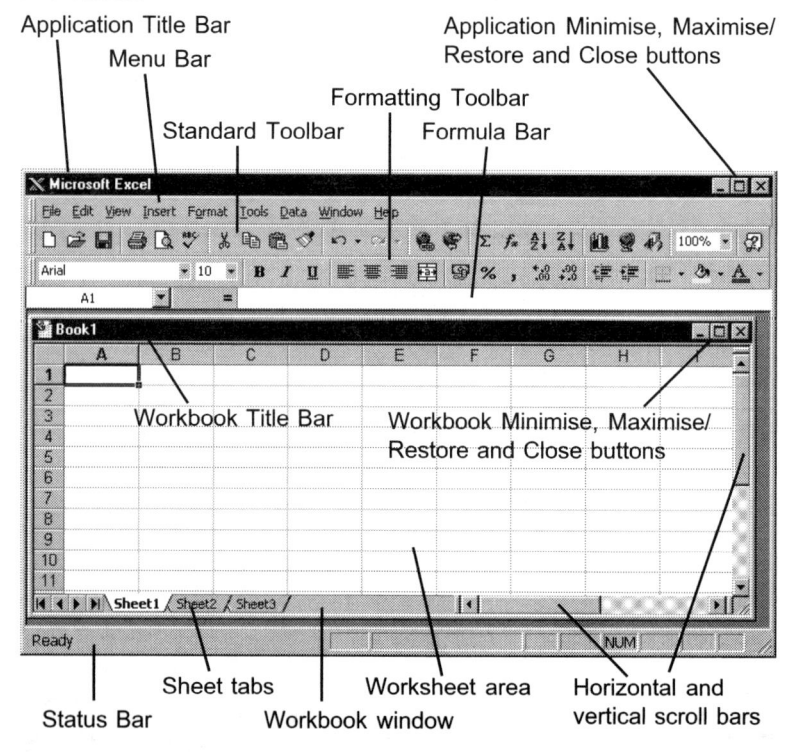

- Application Title Bar
- Menu Bar
- Application Minimise, Maximise/Restore and Close buttons
- Formatting Toolbar
- Standard Toolbar
- Formula Bar
- Workbook Title Bar
- Workbook Minimise, Maximise/Restore and Close buttons
- Sheet tabs
- Status Bar
- Worksheet area
- Workbook window
- Horizontal and vertical scroll bars

If the Workbook window is maximised, the Workbook and the Application share one Title Bar containing the Application and Workbook names.

GETTING STARTED

You'll find the different screen areas referred to by their 'proper' names in the on-line help, throughout this book and in other publications on the package.

1.7 Workbooks and worksheets

When working in Excel, the files that you create and work with are called **workbooks**. Each workbook consists of a number of **worksheets** (the default number is three). You can add more worksheets to a workbook, or remove any you don't need.

Related data is usually best kept on separate worksheets within the same workbook – this makes it easier to find and manage your data.

For example, if you are responsible for collating regional sales figures, you could record the figures for each region on a separate sheet within the same workbook. Alternatively, you could have a separate workbook for each region and record the monthly or quarterly sales figures on separate sheets within each region's workbook.

Worksheets will be discussed more fully in Chapter 4.

1.8 Menus

There are 9 main menus in your Excel Application Window. You can use these menus to access any function or feature available in Excel. I suggest you have a browse through them to get an idea of what's available – some menu items on the lists may appear familiar to you, some will be new.

You can display a menu list and select menu options using either the mouse or the keyboard.

USING THE MOUSE

1 Click on the menu name to display its list of options
2 Click on the menu item you wish to use

USING THE KEYBOARD

You will notice that each menu name has an underlined character in it.

To open a menu using the keyboard:

- Hold down the **[Alt]** key and press the underlined letter, e.g. **[Alt]-[F]** opens the File menu, **[Alt]-[I]** opens the Insert menu.

Each item in a menu list also has a letter underlined in it.

To select an item from the menu list either:

- Press the underlined letter on your keyboard.

Or

- Use the up and down arrow keys on your keyboard until the item you want is selected, then press the **[Enter]** key.

Once a menu list is displayed, you can press the right or left arrow keys on your keyboard to move from one menu to another.

To close a menu without selecting an item from the list:

- Click the menu name again, click anywhere off the menu list or press the **[Esc]** key on your keyboard.

In addition to the menus, many of the commands can be initiated using the toolbars, keyboard shortcuts or shortcut menus. Each of these areas will be covered as you progress through the book.

1.9 Help!

As you work with Excel you will most probably find that you come a bit unstuck from time to time and need help! There are several ways of getting help – most of them very intuitive and user friendly.

GETTING STARTED

Office Assistant

One of the first things you'll notice when working with any of the Office 97 applications is the Office Assistant. The Office Assistant replaces the Answer Wizard found in Office 95. It displays Help topics and tips through its dialog bubble, rather than a standard dialog box!

- To call on the Office Assistant, press **[F1]** or click the **Office Assistant** tool

The Office Assistant will rush to your aid!

Depending on what you have been doing, the Assistant may display a list of topics that you might be interested in.

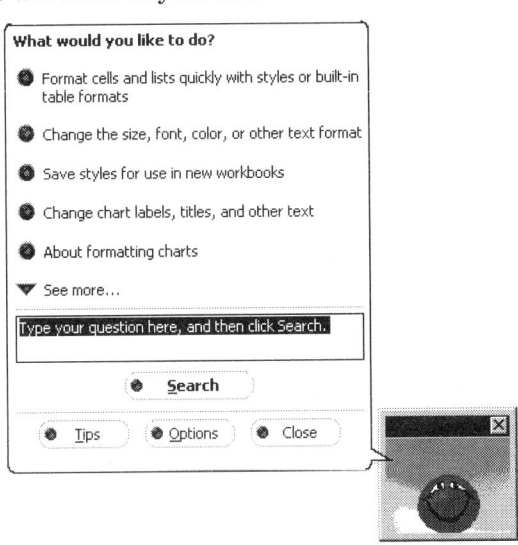

- To choose a topic from the **'What would you like to do?'** list, simply click on the topic.

- If you have a specific question you want to ask, type it in at the prompt and click the **Search** button.

The Assistant will display the Help page requested. Some help pages contain green words or phrases with a dotted green underline – these are technical terms or jargon that may be unfamiliar to you. To find out what the word or phrase means, point to it with the mouse and click.

Click for an explanation

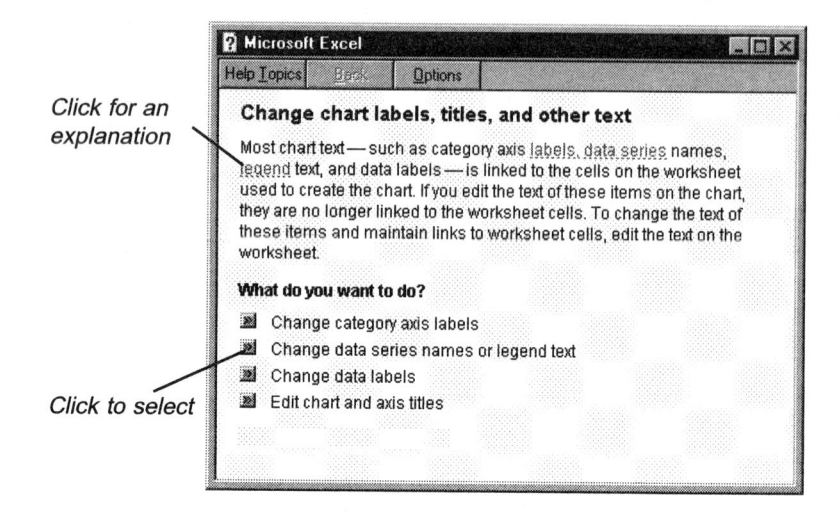

Click to select

> **Change chart labels, titles, and other text**
>
> Most chart text—such as category axis labels, data series names, legend text, and data labels—is linked to the cells on the worksheet used to create the chart. If you edit the text of these items on the chart, they are no longer linked to the worksheet cells. To change the text of these items and maintain links to worksheet cells, edit the text on the worksheet.
>
> **What do you want to do?**
>
> - Change category axis labels
> - Change data series names or legend text
> - Change data labels
> - Edit chart and axis titles

Any related pages will be cross-referenced at the end of the Help page – to display a related page simply click on its cross-reference.

When you've finished exploring the Help system, click the **Close** button at the top right of the Help window.

The Office Assistant window can be left open as you work on your workbook, or you can close it and call on it as required. If you opt to leave it open, drag it (using its title bar) to an area of your screen where it doesn't obscure your work.

- If you leave the Office Assistant window open, click on it any time you want to ask a question.

- To close the Office Assistant window, click the **Close** button on its Title Bar.

To customise the Office Assistant

You can customise the Office Assistant to take on a different appearance, or behave in a different way.

1 Open the Office Assistant
2 Click the **Options** button

3 To change its appearance, select the **Gallery** tab and browse through the options available (use the **Next** and **Back** buttons to move through the various guises)

- If you find an Assistant you would like to use, click **OK**.
- To leave the Assistant as it was, click **Cancel**.

4 To change its behaviour, select the **Options** tab, select or deselect the options available – click on an option to switch it on or off

- A tick in a box means an option is selected, an empty box means it isn't.
- Click **OK** to set the options selected or **Cancel** to leave things as they were.

Tips

The Office Assistant is constantly monitoring your actions. If it thinks that it has a tip that may be useful to you, a light bulb will light up in its window. To read its tip, click the bulb.

If the Tips button is active in the Office Assistant dialog bubble, you can click it and then view the list of tips on offer.

What's This?

If you haven't used Microsoft Office products before, or if you're new to the Windows environment, there will be many tools, menus, buttons and areas on the screen that puzzle you. Help is at hand however – if you don't know what something is just ask. The What's This feature works best when a workbook is open as most of the tools, menus and screen areas are active.

To find out what a tool does:
1 Hold down the **[Shift]** key and press **[F1]**
- The mouse pointer looks like this ▶?
2 Click the tool

To find out about an item in a menu list:

1 Hold down the **[Shift]** key and press **[F1]**
2 Open the menu list
3 Select the option required from the list

To find out about anything else in the application window:

1 Hold down the **[Shift]** key and press **[F1]**
2 Click on the item

If you accidentally invoke the What's This help option, press the **[Esc]** key or **[Shift]-[F1]** to cancel it.

Contents and Index

To get help through the Help menu:

1 Open the **Help** menu
2 Choose **Contents and Index**
3 At the **Help Topics** dialog box, select a tab from which to work – Contents, Index or Find

CONTENTS TAB

You can browse through the Help system from the Contents tab.

- Double click on a book to display or hide its list of contents.

Depending on the book you select, you may be presented with more books, a list of topics, or a mixture of both.

To display a topic:

1 Double click on it
2 Work through the Help system to find the help you need

To print a topic:

1 Select the topic on the **Contents** tab
2 Click **Print...**

Or

GETTING STARTED

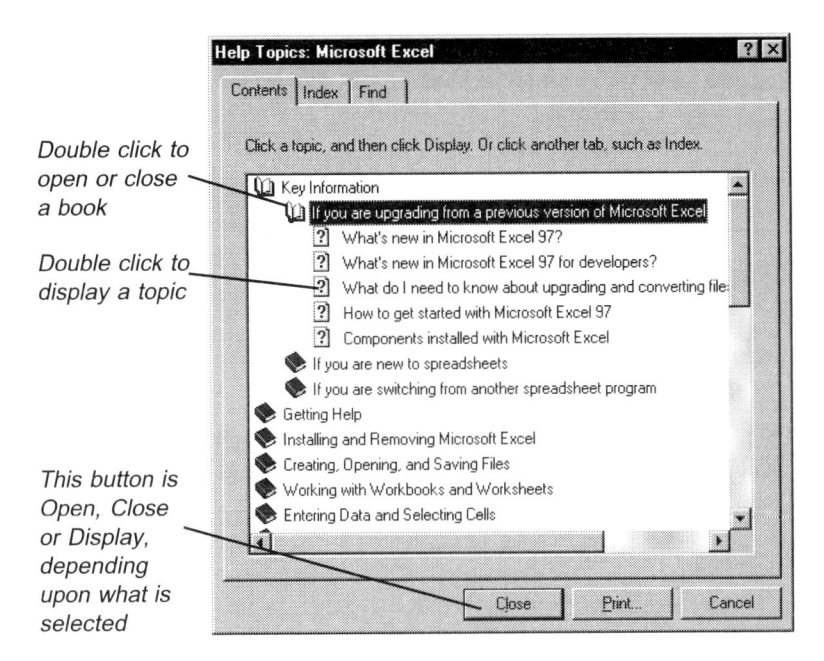

Double click to open or close a book

Double click to display a topic

This button is Open, Close or Display, depending upon what is selected

1 Display the topic – double click on it
2 Click the **Options** button
3 Choose **Print Topic**

• Close the Help window when you're finished.

INDEX TAB

If you know what you are looking for, the Index tab gives you quick access to any topic and is particularly useful once you are familiar with the terminology used in Excel.

1 Choose **Contents and Index** from the Help menu
2 At the **Help Topics** dialog box, select the **Index** tab
3 Start typing in the word you're looking for
4 When the index entry appears in the list, select it
5 Click **Display**

6 A list of related topics will be displayed or the Help text requested will appear (exactly what appears depends on what you have selected from the index)

7 Continue until you find the Help you need

8 Close the Help window when you've finished

Find Tab

The first time you use the Find tab the Find Setup Wizard runs to set up the word list – just follow the prompts to set up your list (this only happens once).

The Find tab is used to search out specific words and phrases, rather than look for a particular category of information.

1 Choose **Contents and Index** from the **Help** menu

2 Select the **Find** tab

3 Type in your word (or part of it – enough to get some matching words displayed)

4 Select a matching word to narrow the search

5 Double click on the topic you wish to display

6 Close the Help window when you're finished

ScreenTips

If you point to any tool on a displayed toolbar, a ScreenTip will probably appear to describe the purpose of the tool.

If no ScreenTips appear, you can easily switch them on if you want to.

To switch ScreenTips on or off:

1 Point to any toolbar and click the *right* mouse button

2 Choose **Customize...** from the shortcut menu

3 In the **Customize** dialog box select the **Options** tab

GETTING STARTED

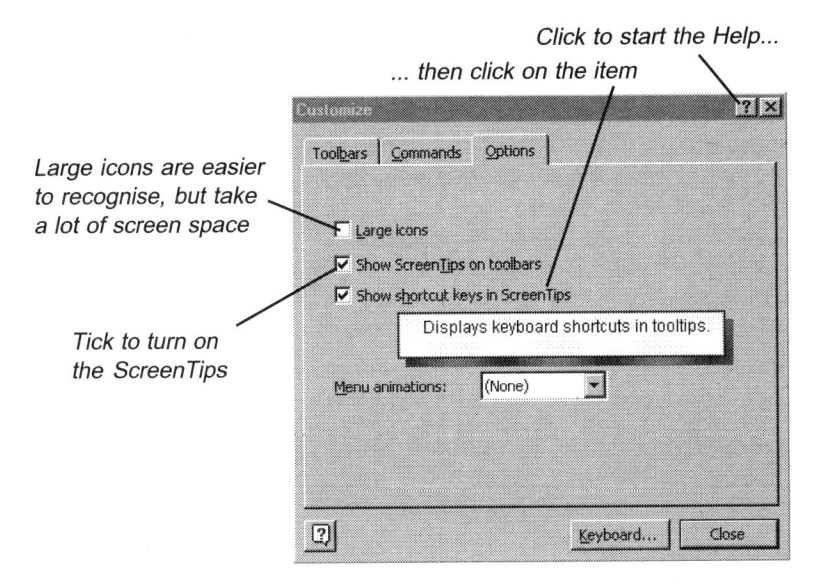

Click to start the Help...
... then click on the item

Large icons are easier to recognise, but take a lot of screen space

Tick to turn on the ScreenTips

> Displays keyboard shortcuts in tooltips.

4 To switch the ScreenTips on, select the **Show ScreenTips on toolbars** option (if you don't like ScreenTips, deselect this option to switch them off)

5 Click **Close**

Dialog Box Help

When you access a dialog box in Excel, e.g. the Customize one above, you can get help on any item within it that you don't understand. To get help on an item in a dialog box:

1 Click the Help button at the right-hand edge of the dialog box title bar

2 Click on an option, button or item in the dialog box that you want explained

- A brief explanation of the option, button or item you click on will be displayed. Click anywhere within the dialog box to cancel the explanation.

1.10 Exiting Excel 97

When you have finished working in Excel you must close the application down – don't just switch off your computer!

To exit Excel:

- Open the **File** menu and choose **Exit**.

Or

- Click the **Close** button in the right-hand corner of the Application title bar.

If you have been working on a workbook, but have not saved it, you will be prompted to do so – see *Save Workbook* in Chapter 2.

1.11 Summary

This chapter has introduced you to Excel 97. We have discussed:

- The fact that Excel 97 is a very powerful, yet easy to use, spreadsheet package.
- The minimum software and hardware requirements necessary to run the package successfully.
- The installation procedure for Excel 97.
- Accessing the package through the Start menu and the Shortcut Bar.
- The Excel screen.
- The difference between a workbook and a worksheet.
- Utilising the menu system using the mouse and the keyboard.
- The Office Assistant and On-line Help system.
- Exiting Excel.

2

BASIC EXCEL SKILLS

2.1 Aims of this chapter

This chapter will introduce you to the basic skills you will need to work in Excel. By the time you have completed this chapter you will have created a simple worksheet and you will know how to create, edit, save, print, open and close a workbook.

2.2 Spreadsheet jargon

Before going any further, spend a little time getting familiar with some of the jargon you will encounter. There's nothing difficult about it – once you know what it means!

ROWS, COLUMNS AND CELLS

The worksheet area consists of rows, columns and cells. Rows are identified by the numbers displayed down the left side of the worksheet area. Row 6 is highlighted in the illustration overleaf. There are lots of rows on a worksheet – 65,536 in fact!

EXCEL 97

Columns are identified by the letters displayed along the top of the worksheet area. Column C is highlighted in the illustration. After Z, columns are labelled AA to AZ, then BA to BZ, and so on to IV, giving 256 columns in all.

Where a row and column intersect you have a cell. Each of the rectangular areas on your worksheet is a cell. Cells are identified using a cell name or 'address'. A cell address consists of the column letter followed by the row number of the column and row that intersect to create the cell. Cells A1, B9, C3, D6 and F3 have been highlighted in the screenshot below.

BASIC EXCEL SKILLS

TEXT, DATA, FORMULAS AND FUNCTIONS

The cells in your worksheet will eventually contain text, numeric data, formulas or functions.

Text is used for titles or narrative to describe the figures you are presenting – worksheet headings, column headings and row labels will usually be text entries.

Numeric data means the figures that appear in your worksheet. The data may be entered through the keyboard, or it may be generated as the result of a calculation.

Formulas are used to perform calculations on the numeric data in your worksheet. Formulas are used, for example, to add the value in one cell to that in another or multiply the values in different cells. Some of your formulas will be very basic, others may be quite complex.

Functions are predefined formulas that perform simple or complex calculations on your data. There are many different kinds of functions set up in Excel – statistical, logical, financial, database, engineering – and many more. You're bound to find some useful ones, whatever type of data you work with.

2.3 Moving around your worksheet

Before you can enter anything into a cell, you must make the cell you want to work on active. To make a single cell active, you must select it. You can easily move onto any cell (thus making it active) using either the keyboard or the mouse.

The active cell has a dark border. The address of the active cell appears in the **Name box** to the left of the Formula bar.

To make a cell active:

Using the mouse

- Click on the cell (you may need to use the horizontal or vertical scrollbars to bring the cell into view if it isn't on the screen).

Using the keyboard

- Use the right and left arrow keys on your keyboard to move right or left one column at a time.
- Use the up and down arrow keys on your keyboard to move up or down one row at a time.
- Press the **[Enter]** key to move onto the cell directly below the one that is currently active.

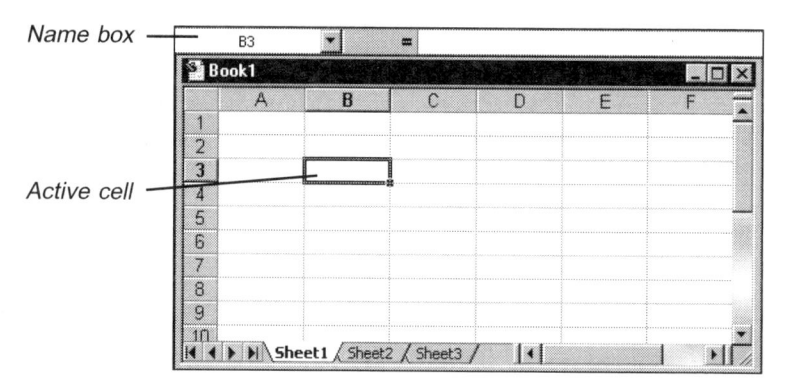

Name box

Active cell

You can also go to a specific cell, if you know the address of the cell you want to go to.

To go to a specific cell:

1. Press the **[F5]** key on your keyboard
2. Enter the address of the cell you want to go to in the Reference field of the **Go To** dialog box
3. Click **OK**

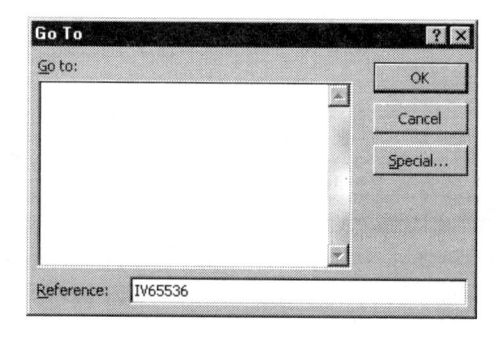

BASIC EXCEL SKILLS

To return to cell A1 from anywhere in your worksheet:
- Hold down the [**Ctrl**] key and press [**Home**].

To move to the end of the work area on your worksheet (the last cell you worked on, rather than cell IV65536):
- Hold down the [**Ctrl**] key and press [**End**].

Check out Keyboard shortcuts in the on-line Help, to see if there are any others that you would find useful.

2.4 Selection techniques

You will find that you often work on more than one cell at a time in Excel. You may need to format a group of cells in a particular way or copy or move a group of cells, or apply a function to a group of cells.

A group of cells is called a *cell range*. Cell ranges are identified by using the first cell address followed by the last cell address in the group. A1:A7, C3:D12 and F5:H7 are highlighted in the picture below. Note that the cell addresses are separated by a colon, and there are no spaces in the expression.

You can select a range using either the mouse or the keyboard.

USING THE MOUSE

To select a group of adjacent cells:

- *Click and drag*

1 Click and drag over the range of cells you wish to select

Or

- *Click-[Shift]-click*

1 Click on a cell in one corner of the range you wish to select
2 Hold the **[Shift]** key down on your keyboard
3 Click on the cell in the diagonally opposite corner of the range

To select a row or rows:

- Click the row number in the far-left column.

Or

- Click and drag down over the row numbers to select several rows.

To select a column or columns:

- Click the column letter at the top of the column.

Or

- Click and drag across the letters to select several columns.

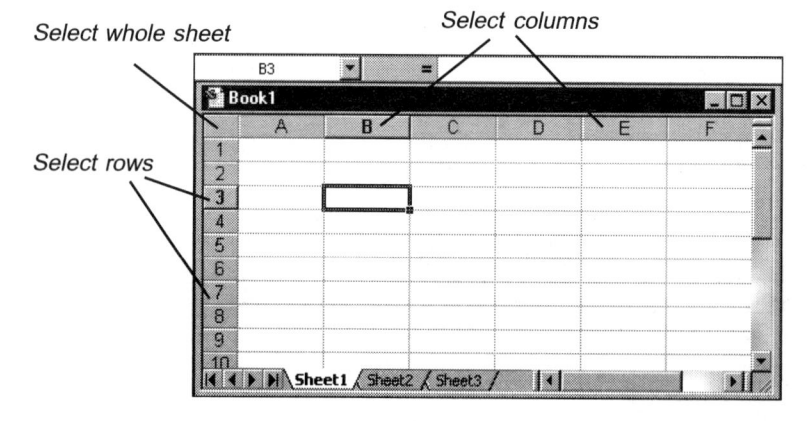

Select whole sheet

Select columns

Select rows

BASIC EXCEL SKILLS

To select the whole worksheet:
- Click the box at the top of the row numbers, and left of the column letters.

To select a range of non-adjacent cells:
1. Click on one of the cells you want to select
2. Hold the [Ctrl] key down
3. Click on each of the other cells you want to select

To de-select a range of cells:
- Click on any cell in your worksheet.

USING THE KEYBOARD

To select a group of adjacent cells:
1. Click in a cell that will be in the corner of the range you wish to select
2. Hold the [Shift] key down
3. Press the arrow keys on your keyboard to move to the cell in the corner diagonally opposite the one clicked on at step 1

To de-select a range of cells:
- Press one of the arrow keys on your keyboard.

2.5 Entering text and data

Entering text or data into your worksheet is easy.

1. Select the cell you want to enter text or data into
2. Type in the text or data – the text or data will appear in the Formula bar as well as in the active cell
3. Move on to the next cell you want to make active – press [Enter], or press the arrow keys on your keyboard, click on a different cell or click the 'tick' button to the left of the Formula bar

EXCEL 97

Things to note when entering text:
- Text that doesn't fit into a single cell will spill over into the next cell if the column is empty.
- Text that doesn't fit into a single cell appears to be chopped off if there is something in the cell to the right.
- Text automatically aligns to the left of a cell.

Things to note when entering numeric data:
- If you have adjusted the width of a column (see 2.7 below) then enter data that is too large for the column width the cell will display ######## signs instead of the figures. When this happens you must either change the number format (see 2.9) or adjust the column width again (see 2.7).

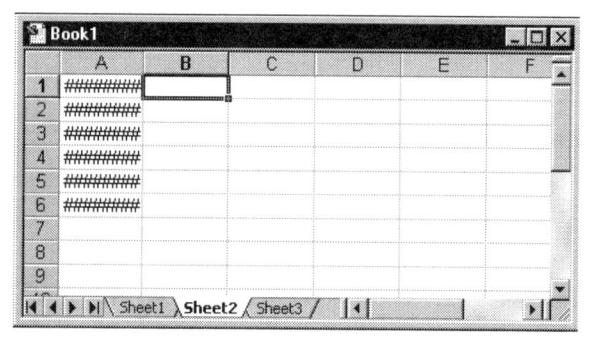

- Numeric data automatically aligns to the right of a cell.

2.6 Editing text and data

If you make an error when entering your work, you can fix things by:
- Deleting the contents of the cell.
- Replacing the contents of the cell.
- Editing the contents of the cell.

BASIC EXCEL SKILLS

To delete the contents of a cell (or cells):

1 Select the cell (or cells) whose contents you want to erase

2 Press the **[Delete]** key on your keyboard

To replace the contents of a cell:

1 Select the cell whose contents you want to replace

2 Type in the text or data that should be in the cell

To edit the contents of a cell:

1 Select the cell whose contents you want to edit

2 Click in the Formula bar to place the insertion point in it

3 Edit the cell contents as required (you can move right and left using the arrow keys, delete using the **[Delete]** or **[Backspace]** key, or enter text or data through the keyboard)

4 Press **[Enter]** on your keyboard when you've finished editing

Or

1 Double click in the cell whose contents you want to edit – this places the insertion point within the cell

2 Edit the cell contents as required

3 Press **[Enter]** on your keyboard when you've finished editing

---

EXAMPLES IN THIS BOOK

Throughout this book we will use several different worksheets to illustrate various features in Excel. I suggest you enter these examples into a workbook and use them as practice material. You can then follow the instructions in the book and experiment with the features.

SIMON'S SPORTSHOP

The first worksheet will display a list of items that are in a sale in Simon's Sportshop. Enter the text displayed in the worksheet below and build up the worksheet as you work through the rest of the chapter.

2.7 Column width

If the text you are entering into a cell is more than the column width will accommodate, you must do something about it.

Sometimes – particularly with main headings at the top of a worksheet – it doesn't matter if the text you enter spills over into the cells to the right. However, when entering column headings or row labels each entry should occupy a single cell – with no overspill into the next column.

One way to make text fit into a single cell is to adjust the column width as necessary.

Text spilling over into adjacent cell

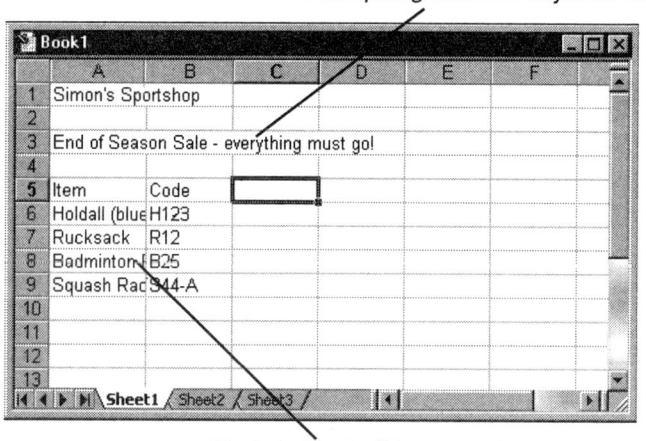

Text chopped off because the next cell is occupied

MANUAL ADJUSTMENT

To change the width of a column:

- In the column heading row, click and drag the vertical line to the right of the column whose width you want to change – in this example we need to widen column A.

AUTOFIT

You can get Excel to automatically adjust the width of the column to fit the entries within it.

Click and drag to widen column

	A	B	C	D	E	F
1	Simon's Sportshop					
2						
3	End of Season Sale - everything must go!					
4						
5	Item	Code				
6	Holdall (blue Nylon)	H123				
7	Rucksack	R12				
8	Badminton Racket	B25				
9	Squash Racket	S44-A				
10						
11						
12						
13						

To adjust the column width automatically:

- In the column-heading row, double click the vertical line to the right of the column you want to adjust.

FORMAT MENU

You can also adjust the column width from the Format menu.

To set a specific column width using the Format menu:

1 Select any cell in the column you want to adjust
2 Open the **Format** menu and choose **Column**
3 Choose **Width**
4 Enter the size required at the **Column Width** dialog box
5 Click **OK**

To automatically adjust the column width from the Format menu:

1 Select the cell that will determine the column width required for your column
2 Open the **Format** menu and choose **Column**
3 Click **AutoFit Selection**

To change the default column width for your columns:

1 Open the **Format** menu and choose **Column**

2 Choose **Standard Width**

3 At the **Standard Width** dialog box, enter the size required

4 Click **OK**

———2.8 Text wrap within a cell———

There are times when it is best to force a text entry to wrap within a cell, rather than have to widen a column to accommodate it. This particularly applies to column headings. Consequently it may be useful to set the *text wrap within cell* option for the row that contains the column headings in your worksheet.

In the example below, monetary values will eventually go in the *Recommended Retail Price* column, and the monetary entries will only take up 6 or 7 characters. To widen the column to accommodate "Recommended Retail Price" would result in a rather strange looking layout in our final worksheet.

Widening makes column too wide

	A	B	C	D	E
1	Simon's Sportshop				
2					
3	End of Season Sale - everything must go!				
4					
5	Item	Code	Recommended Retail Price	Sale Price	Saving
6	Holdall (blue Nylon)	H123			
7	Rucksack	R12			
8	Badminton Racket	B25			
9	Squash Racket	S44-A			

To specify that text should wrap within a row of cells:

1 Select the row you want to set the text wrap option for
2 Open the **Format** menu and choose **Cells...**
3 Select the **Alignment** tab
4 Select the **Wrap text** checkbox
5 Click **OK**

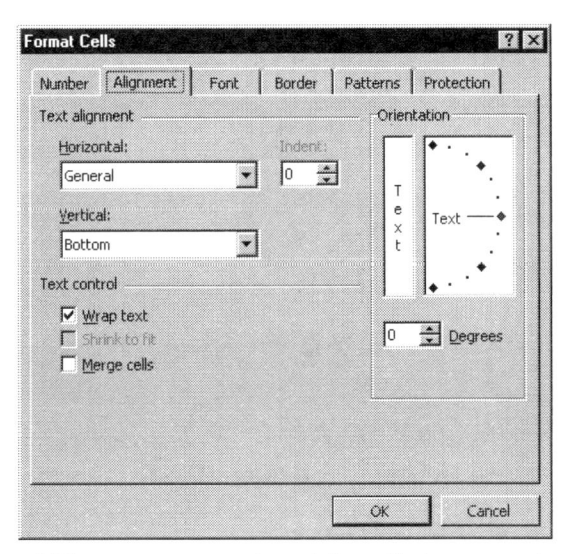

Adjust the column widths as necessary to get the effect you want.

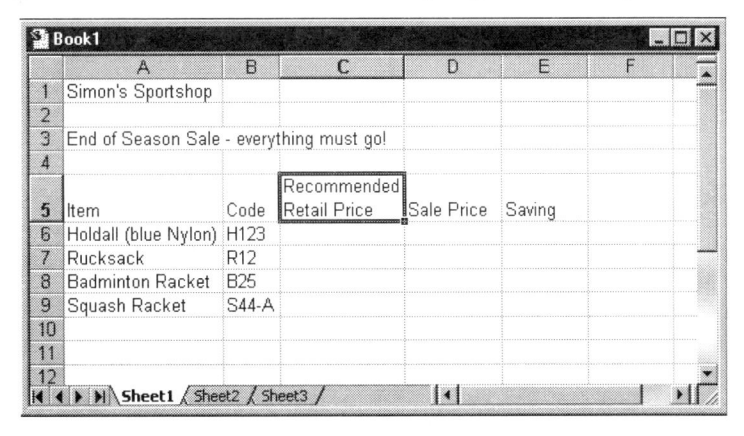

- If the row height does not adjust automatically to accommodate the text when it wraps, choose **Row** from the **Format** menu, then select **AutoFit**.

Shrink to fit

If the contents of a cell are just too wide for the column width, and you don't want to widen the column, you can get the contents of the cell to 'shrink to fit'.

1. Select the cell whose contents you want to shrink to fit
2. Open the **Format** menu and choose **Cells...**
3. On the **Alignment** tab, select the **Shrink to Fit** checkbox and click **OK**

2.9 Number formats

A lot of the data entered into a worksheet is currency. Most of the times that you enter currency values, you will want the appropriate currency symbol to precede the figure – usually, but not always, a £ sign.

If you want the £ sign in front of a figure you can either:

- Format the cells to display the entry in a currency format.

Or

- Enter the £ sign through the keyboard.

If you enter figures through the numeric keypad, it's probably easiest to format the cells to display the figures as currency.

You can format cells before or after you have entered your text or data.

To display the figures in currency format:
1. Select the cells you want to format (see 2.4 above)
2. Click the **Currency** tool on the **Formatting** toolbar

BASIC EXCEL SKILLS

	A	B	C	D	E
1	Simon's Sportshop				
2					
3	End of Season Sale - everything must go!				
4					
5	Item	Code	Recommended Retail Price	Sale Price	Saving
6	Holdall (blue Nylon)	H123	£ 15.50	£ 9.99	
7	Rucksack	R12	£ 16.99	£ 9.99	
8	Badminton Racket	B25	£ 24.00	£ 15.66	
9	Squash Racket	S44-A	£ 27.75	£ 19.99	

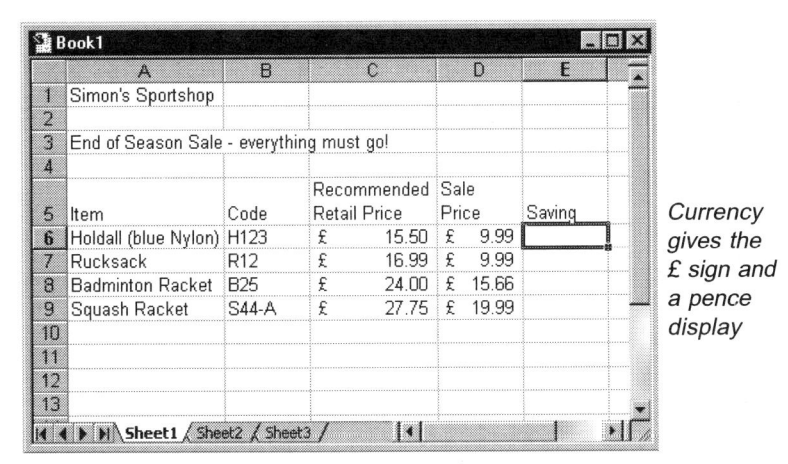

Currency gives the £ sign and a pence display

The Formatting toolbar has other tools to help you format your numbers – Percent, Comma, Increase and Decrease Decimal. Other number formats can be found in the Format Cells dialog box, on the Number tab – see if any would be useful to you.

To apply a format from the Format Cells dialog box:

1. Select the cells you want to format
2. Open the **Format** menu and choose **Cells...**
3. Select the **Number** tab
4. Choose a category from the list
5. Complete the dialog box as required – exactly what appears in it depends on the category you select
6. Click **OK**

2.10 Formulas

Any cell in your workbook which will contain a figure that has been calculated using other entries in your workbook should have a formula or function in it (do not do your calculations on a calculator, then type the answer in to your workbook).

Formulas allow you to add, subtract, multiply, divide and work out percentages of the values in cells.

The operators used in formulas are:

+ Add - Subtract
/ Divide * Multiply
% Percentage

In our example we are going to use a formula to work out how much a customer will save if they buy something out of the sale.

To work out the saving for the first item in the list (the holdall), we need to subtract the sale price (the figure in cell D6) from the recommended retail price (the figure in cell C6).

The result of this calculation should be displayed in cell E6 – in the Saving column.

To enter the formula required:

1 Select the cell that will contain the formula (E6 in this case)

2 Press the [=] key (to tell Excel we're entering a formula)

3 Click on cell C6 (the recommended retail price cell)

- The cell address appears in the Formula bar and the current cell.

4 Press the [–] key on your keyboard (we're subtracting)

5 Click on cell D6 (the cell that contains the sale price figure)

6 Press [**Enter**] on your keyboard

- The result of the calculation will appear in cell E6.

At step 3 and step 5 above, I suggested you click on the cell you want in your formula. If you prefer, you can enter the cell address manually by typing the co-ordinates into your formula instead.

Simple formula examples

=A7/B6   Divide the figure in A7 by the figure in B6

=D22*12   Multiply the figure in D22 by 12

=C7*25%   Calculate 25% of the figure in C7

BASIC EXCEL SKILLS

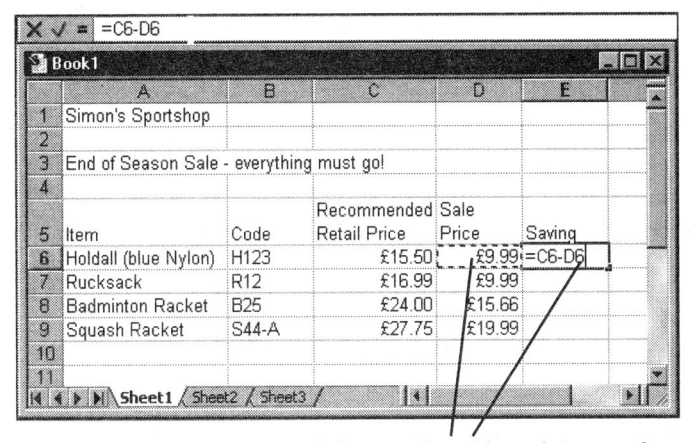

Click on a cell to get its address into your formula

Order of precedence

If there is a mixture of operators in a formula, Excel will deal with multiplication and division before it deals with addition and subtraction – the normal order of priority for arithmetic.

=A4+C7*D7   Multiply the figure in C7 by the one in D7, and add the answer to the figure in A4

=A1+B2/C3+D4*E5-F2   Add to the figure in A1, the result of dividing the figure in B2 by that in C3, then add the result of multiplying the figure in D4 by that in E5, then subtract the figure in F2 (phew!!)

Parentheses

Some formulas can become quite long and complicated – and tricky to follow!

If you want to force the order in which a formula is worked out, or even just make a long formula easier to read, you must use parentheses ( ).

In the next example, the problem within each set of parentheses is solved before working through the formula.

– 33 –

=(A1+B2)/C3+(D4*(E5-F2))

Add A1 to B2	we'll call this XX
Subtract F2 from E5	we'll call this YY
Multiply YY by D4	we'll call this ZZ
Divide XX by C3 then add ZZ	and that is the answer

I hope you followed that!

2.11 AutoFill

In the sportshop sale worksheet, we could work down the column entering the formula for each saving cell as described in 2.10 above. However, a much quicker way to achieve the same result is to use the AutoFill option. AutoFill allows you to copy a formula from one cell into adjacent cells – to the right, left, up or down.

To AutoFill the formula in E6 to the other cells in the Saving column:

1 Select E6

2 Position the mouse pointer over the bottom right corner of the cell – the Fill Handle should appear – a small black cross

3 Click and drag the cross down over the other saving cells

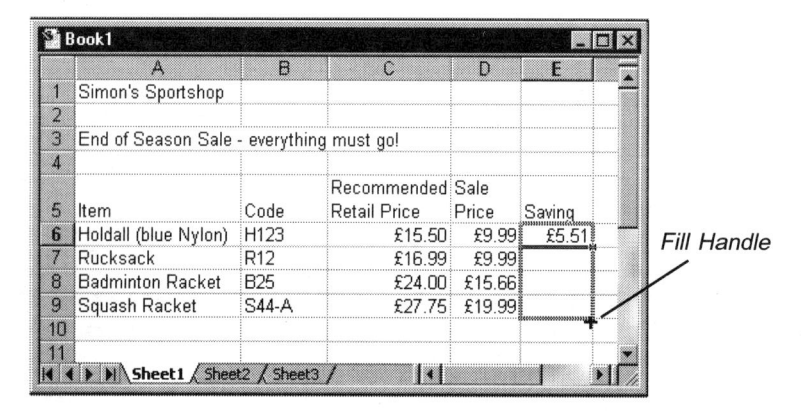

	A	B	C	D	E
1	Simon's Sportshop				
2					
3	End of Season Sale - everything must go!				
4					
5	Item	Code	Recommended Retail Price	Sale Price	Saving
6	Holdall (blue Nylon)	H123	£15.50	£9.99	£5.51
7	Rucksack	R12	£16.99	£9.99	
8	Badminton Racket	B25	£24.00	£15.66	
9	Squash Racket	S44-A	£27.75	£19.99	

Fill Handle

BASIC EXCEL SKILLS

When you let go the mouse, the formula in cell E6 will be copied to the cells you dragged over.

If you click on each cell in the saving column and keep an eye on the Formula bar, you will notice that Excel has automatically changed the cell addresses in the formula relative to the position you have copied the formula to. Neat trick!

AutoFill can be a real time saver in some situations. Try these.

If you need to enter column or row labels for each month of the year or day of the week:

1 Enter the first month or day you want to use into the appropriate cell – 'January' or 'Jan', 'September' or 'Sept', 'Wednesday' or 'Wed'

2 AutoFill the contents of that cell across the columns or down the rows

- Excel will automatically complete the other cells.

If you need to enter a row or columns of numbers in sequence e.g. 1, 2, 3, 4 etc or 50, 100, 150, etc:

1 Enter the first two numbers in two adjacent cells

2 Select both cells

3 AutoFill down the rows or across the columns

If you want to enter dates, you can use the **Fill** option. The date can be incremented using every day of the week (day), weekdays only (Monday to Friday), months or years.

1 Enter the first date in your series

2 Click and drag the Fill Handle using the *right* mouse button

3 When you let go, a pop-up menu appears

4 Select the fill option you require – **Fill Days**, **Fill Weekdays**, **Fill Months** or **Fill Years**

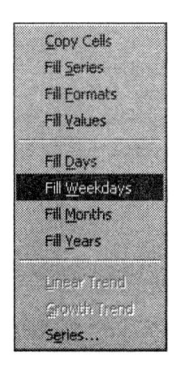

Examples of some of the fill options are displayed below.

	A	B	C	D	E	F	G
1					Step value 10	Fill Years	Fill weekdays
2	JAN	January	Monday	Mon	10	01/01/97	01/12/97
3	FEB	February	Tuesday	Tue	20	01/01/98	02/12/97
4	MAR	March	Wednesday	Wed	30	01/01/99	03/12/97
5	APR	April	Thursday	Thu	40	01/01/00	04/12/97
6	MAY	May	Friday	Fri	50	01/01/01	05/12/97
7	JUN	June	Saturday	Sat	60	01/01/02	08/12/97
8	JUL	July	Sunday	Sun	70	01/01/03	09/12/97
9	AUG	August	Monday	Mon	80	01/01/04	10/12/97
10	SEP	September	Tuesday	Tue	90	01/01/05	11/12/97
11	OCT	October	Wednesday	Wed		01/01/06	12/12/97
12	NOV	November	Thursday	Thu		01/01/07	
13	DEC	December	Friday	Fri		01/01/08	
14	JAN		Saturday	Sat		01/01/09	

- Column A and B show different month formats AutoFilled.
- Column C and D show different day formats AutoFilled.
- Column E shows figures with an increment of 10 AutoFilled.
- Column F has been completed using the Fill Years option on the pop-up menu.
- Column G has been completed using the Fill Weekdays option on the pop-up menu.

2.12 Another worksheet!

Use this example to get some more practice. Enter the text and data below into a new worksheet in your workbook. To select a different sheet, click the sheet tab – *Sheet1*, *Sheet2*, etc. to the left of the horizontal scroll bar. It doesn't matter what sheet you use. This example is for a stock value table for *Screw the nut plc*.

Use these notes to help you get the layout and formulas correct.

- Enter the main headings and column headings – 'Part No', 'Description', 'Cost (trade)', 'Cost (retail)', 'Profit', 'Number in Stock' and 'Value of Stock'.

- Format row 5 to allow text wrap within the cells (see 2.8 above).
- Format the data cells in the *Cost (trade)*, *Cost (retail)*, *Profit* and *Value of Stock* columns to display the figures as currency (see 2.9 above).
- Enter a formula to calculate the *Profit* figure. For the first item (the screwdriver set), it would be **=D6–C6** (see 2.10 above for information on entering formulas).
- Enter a formula to calculate the *Value of Stock* column. For the first item it would be **=D6*F6** (if you base the stock value on the retail price rather than the trade price of the item).
- AutoFill the formulas down the columns (see 2.11 above).
- The *Total value of stock* figure could be calculated by entering the formula **=G6+G7+G8+G9** (you could use the AutoSum function for this – see 5.2).

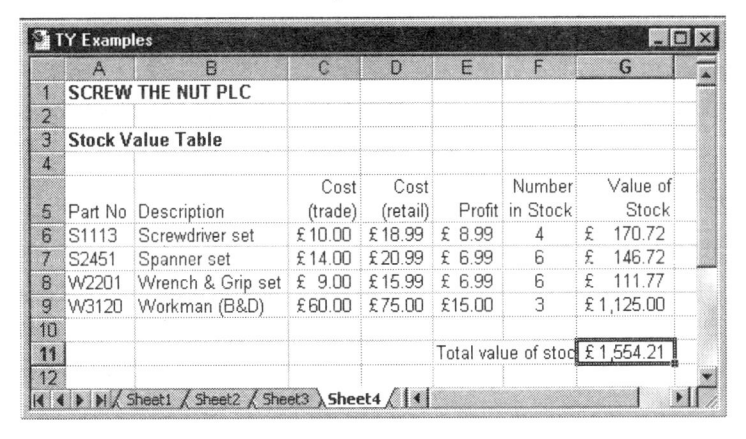

	A	B	C	D	E	F	G
1	SCREW THE NUT PLC						
2							
3	Stock Value Table						
4							
5	Part No	Description	Cost (trade)	Cost (retail)	Profit	Number in Stock	Value of Stock
6	S1113	Screwdriver set	£ 10.00	£ 18.99	£ 8.99	4	£ 170.72
7	S2451	Spanner set	£ 14.00	£ 20.99	£ 6.99	6	£ 146.72
8	W2201	Wrench & Grip set	£ 9.00	£ 15.99	£ 6.99	6	£ 111.77
9	W3120	Workman (B&D)	£ 60.00	£ 75.00	£ 15.00	3	£ 1,125.00
10							
11						Total value of stock	£ 1,554.21
12							

2.13 Moving or copying cells

If you enter text or data into your worksheet, and it's correct but in the wrong place, you can move it to where it should be (rather than delete it and retype it in the correct location).

To move the contents of cells:

1 Select the cells you want to move

2 Click the **Cut** tool on the Standard toolbar

3 Select the top leftmost cell of the range you want to move the text or data to

4 Click the **Paste** tool on the Standard toolbar

Or

1 Select the cells you want to move

2 Point to the edge of the selected area – the mouse pointer becomes a white pointer shape

3 Drag and drop the selected cells in the correct position

To copy the contents of cells:

1 Select the cells you want to copy

2 Click the **Copy** tool on the Standard toolbar

• Note the dotted line that appears around the cells to be copied.

3 Select the top leftmost cell of the range you want to copy the text or data to

4 Click the **Paste** tool on the Standard toolbar

• If you want more than one copy, repeat steps 3 and 4 until you've all the copies required.

5 Press **[Esc]** to cancel the dotted line around the copied cells

Or

1 Select the cells you want to move

2 Point to the edge of the selected area – the mouse pointer becomes a white pointer shape

3 Hold down the **[Ctrl]** key while you drag and drop the selected cells. Make sure you let go the mouse button before the **[Ctrl]** key – if you don't you'll move the cells instead of copying them.

BASIC EXCEL SKILLS

2.14 Adjusting rows and columns

As you build up your worksheet, you may discover that you have added a row or column that you don't require, or perhaps missed out a row or column that you do need.

To insert a row:
1 Select the row that will go below the row you are inserting
2 Right click within the selected area
3 Choose **Insert** from the pop-up menu

To insert a column:
1 Select the column that will go to the right of the column you are inserting
2 Right click within the selected area
3 Choose **Insert** from the pop-up menu

To delete a row or column:
1 Select the row or column you wish to delete
2 Right click within the selected area
3 Choose **Delete**

To add or delete several rows or columns at the same time:
1 Click and drag in the row or column label area to indicate the number of rows or columns you want to insert or delete
2 Right click within the selected area
3 Choose **Insert** or **Delete** as required

2.15 Save Workbook

In Excel, a file is called a workbook. Each workbook you create is automatically given a temporary filename – *Book1*, *Book2*, *Book3*, etc. The filename appears on the workbook Title Bar.

At some stage you must save your workbook to disk (if you don't you will lose it when you switch off your computer). When you save your workbook, you should give it a file name that reflects its contents rather than use the *Book1, Book2* temporary name.

You can save your workbook at any time – you don't need to wait until you've entered all your data. I suggest you save your workbook regularly – and remember to resave it when you make changes to it. If you haven't saved you workbook, and your computer crashes or you have a power failure, you may lose any unsaved data.

To save your workbook:

1 Click the **Save** tool 🖬 on the Standard toolbar

2 At the **Save As** dialog box, locate the folder in which you wish to save your workbook (usually My Documents)

3 Enter the file name in the **File name:** field

4 Leave the **Save as type:** field at *Microsoft Excel Workbook*

5 Click **Save**

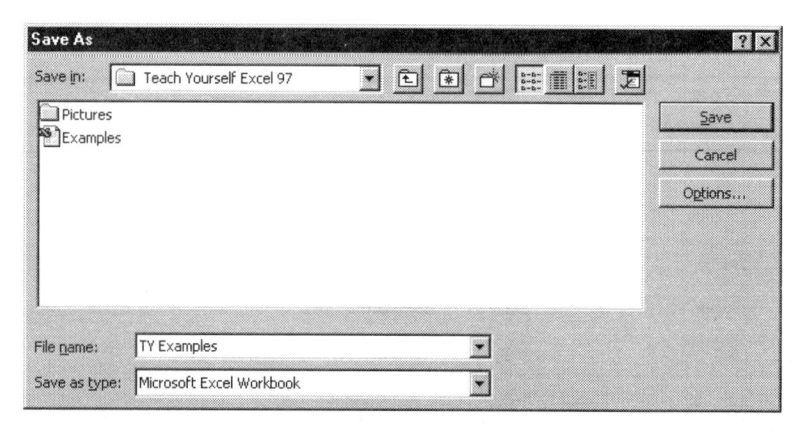

You are returned to your workbook. The name of the workbook appears on the workbook title bar.

You can save your workbook whenever you like. Once a workbook has been saved, simply click the Save tool on the Standard toolbar

The filename is shown in the Title Bar

	A	B	C	D	E	F
1	Simon's Sportshop					
2						
3	End of Season Sale - everything must go!					
4						
5	Item	Code	Recommended Retail Price	Sale Price	Saving	
6	Holdall (blue Nylon)	H123	£15.50	£9.99	£5.51	
7	Rucksack	R12	£16.99	£9.99	£7.00	
8	Badminton Racket	B25	£24.00	£15.66	£8.34	
9	Squash Racket	S44-A	£27.75	£19.99	£7.76	
10						

when you want to save any changes to it. When you click the Save tool to save a workbook that has already been saved, the Save As dialog box does not reappear, but the up-to-date version of your workbook replaces the old version already saved to disk.

Save As

There may be times that you save a workbook, edit it, then decide that you want to save the edited workbook but also keep the original version of the workbook on disk.

If you don't want to overwrite the old version of your workbook with the new edited version, save the new version using a different file name. You can save your workbook to the same folder if you want to, or you can select a different drive and/or folder.

1 Open the **File** menu and choose **Save As**

2 The **Save As** dialog will appear again

3 Enter a new name in the **File name** field

4 Click **Save**

- If you save the new version of the file into the same folder as the old one, you must use a different file name.

2.16 Print Preview and Print

At some stage you will want to print your file. Before sending a workbook to print, it's a good idea to preview it. It takes practice to get a good fit, to start with, and you may find it useful to plan things in rough before you begin to draw up your worksheet. Page layout options are discussed on in 3.9.

Print Preview

To preview your worksheet:

- Click the **Print Preview** tool on the Standard toolbar.

A preview of the current worksheet will be displayed on your screen, in full-page view.

It doesn't matter if you can't read what is on the screen – the preview is there to let you see how your worksheet will fit onto your paper. You get an idea of how well the data, graphics, etc. will look on the page.

```
Simon's Sportshop
End of Season Sale - everything must go!

                            Rec
                            Retail  Sale
Item                  Code  Price   Price   Saving
Holdall (blue Nylon)  H123  £15.50  £9.99   £5.51
Rucksack              R12   £16.99  £9.99   £7.00
Badminton Racket      B25   £24.00  £15.66  £8.34
Squash Racket         S44-A £27.75  £19.99  £7.76
```

To change something when you see the preview:

1 Click the **Close** tool on the Print Preview toolbar to return to your worksheet

2 Edit as required

3 Preview again to see how it looks

Print

When you are happy with the preview of your worksheet, you can send it to print.

BASIC EXCEL SKILLS

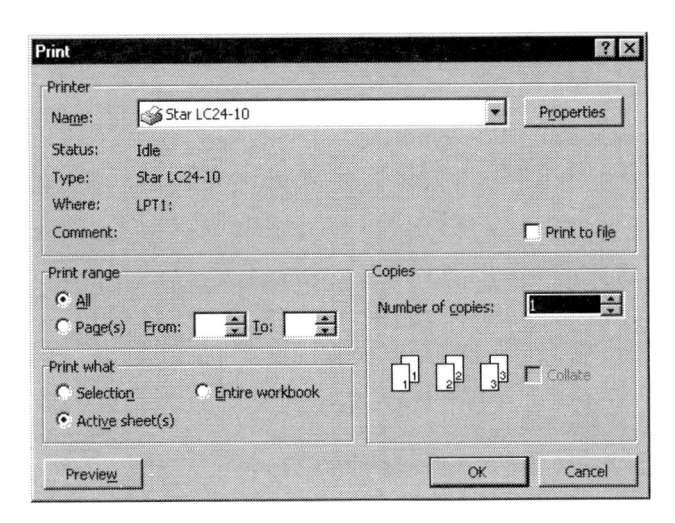

If you are in Print Preview:

1 Click the **Print...** tool on the Print Preview toolbar

2 Complete the **Print** dialog box as required – specify **Number of copies** and **Print range**

3 Click **OK**

If you have your worksheet displayed (not in print preview):

- Click the **Print** tool on the Standard toolbar.

One copy of the current worksheet will be sent to your printer.

If you don't want to print all of your worksheet, you can print the area required on its own.

To print part of your worksheet:

1 Select the range of cells you want to print

2 Open the **File** menu and choose **Print...**

3 Select *Selection* from the **Print what** options

4 Click **OK**

2.17 Close, Open and New

To close your workbook:

- Open the **File** menu and choose **Close**.

Or

- Click the **Close** button in the workbook window.

To open a workbook:

- If the workbook you want to open has been used recently, you may find it in the list of recently-used files in the **File** menu.

1 Click the **Open** tool on the Standard toolbar

Or

- Choose **Open** from the **File** menu.

2 In the **Open** dialog box, locate and select the workbook

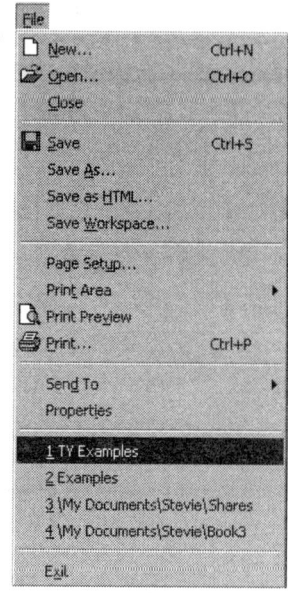

3 Click **Open**

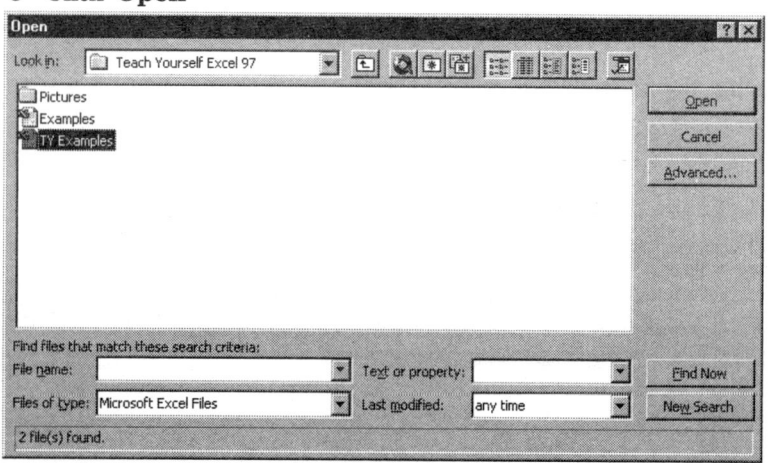

— 44 —

If you want to create a new workbook from within Excel:

- Click the **New** tool on the Standard toolbar.

A new workbook will appear on your screen.

2.18 Summary

In this chapter we have discussed some of the basic skills required when using Excel. We have considered:

- Spreadsheet jargon.
- Moving around a worksheet.
- Cell names and ranges.
- Selection techniques – for rows, columns, adjacent and non-adjacent cells.
- Entering text and data.
- Deleting, replacing and editing the contents of a cell.
- Adjusting column widths.
- Wrapping text within a cell and 'shrink to fit'.
- Number formats.
- Entering simple formula.
- Order of precedence and the use of parentheses.
- AutoFill.
- Moving and copying cells.
- Inserting and deleting rows and columns.
- File handling functions – Save, Print, Close, Open and New.

3

FORMATTING AND LAYOUT

3.1 Aims of this chapter

In this chapter we will consider some of the cell formatting options that you can use to improve the presentation of your worksheet. We will also discuss ways of viewing different areas of your worksheet on the screen at the same time. Finally, to help you get your printouts exactly as you want them, we'll look at some of the page layout options available.

3.2 Bold, italic and underline

You can make the contents of a cell (or cells) bold, italic or underlined using the Formatting toolbar or keyboard shortcuts.

Formatting toolbar

1 Select the cells you wish to make bold, italic or underlined

2 Click the **Bold** tool **B** on the Formatting toolbar to make the cell contents bold

Or

Click the **Italic** tool [*I*] to put the cell contents into italics

Or

Click the **Underline** tool [U] to underline the cell contents

3 Deselect the cells

The bold, italics and underline tools are toggles – they are used to switch the formatting on or off.

To remove formatting from a cell or cells:

1 Select the cell or cells you wish to remove the formatting from
2 Click the Bold, Italic and/or Underline tool on the Formatting toolbar
3 Deselect the cells

Keyboard shortcuts

1 Select the cell or cells you wish to format
2 Apply or remove the formatting with these keyboard shortcuts
- **[Ctrl]-[B]** for bold
- **[Ctrl]-[I]** for italics
- **[Ctrl]-[U]** for underline
3 Deselect the cells

3.3 Alignment

When entering text and data into your worksheet, the default alignment of text within a cell is to the left, the default alignment of numeric data is to the right. You can change the alignment of text or data within a cell if you wish.

Left right and centre

1 Select the cells required

2 Click the **Align Left** tool on the Formatting toolbar to align the cell contents to the left

Or

Click the **Align Center** tool to align to the centre

Or

Click the **Align Right** tool to align to the right

3 Deselect the cells

Merge and Center

If you want to merge cells and centre the data in a cell across them, you can use Merge and Center tool. This option is useful when you want to centre a heading across several columns in your worksheet – perhaps the text in the worksheet title row.

To centre text or data across several columns:

2 Select the range you want to centre the text across, e.g. A3:E3

3 Click the **Merge and Center** tool

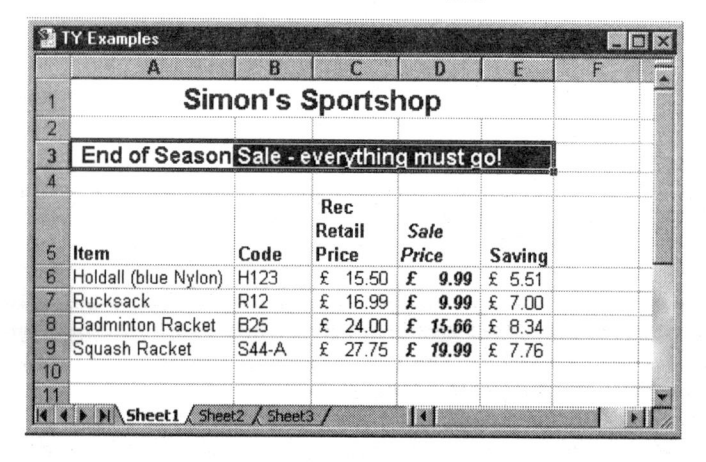

	A	B	C	D	E	F
1		Simon's Sportshop				
2						
3	End of Season	Sale - everything must go!				
4						
5	Item	Code	Rec Retail Price	Sale Price	Saving	
6	Holdall (blue Nylon)	H123	£ 15.50	£ 9.99	£ 5.51	
7	Rucksack	R12	£ 16.99	£ 9.99	£ 7.00	
8	Badminton Racket	B25	£ 24.00	£ 15.66	£ 8.34	
9	Squash Racket	S44-A	£ 27.75	£ 19.99	£ 7.76	
10						
11						

FORMATTING AND LAYOUT

3.4 More formatting options

The default font used in Excel worksheets is Arial, font size 10. You can change the font used or the font size if you wish. The colours of the text or the background can be set as required, and you can add borders to any or all sides of a block of cells if you want to make them really stand out.

To change the font:
1 Select the cells you want to modify
2 Click the drop-down arrow to the right of the **Font** field on the Formatting toolbar
3 Choose an alternative font from the list (use the scroll bar if necessary to bring the font required into view)

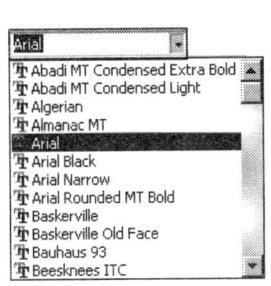

To change the font size:
1 Select the cells you want to modify
2. Click the drop-down arrow to the right of the **Font Size** field on the Formatting toolbar
3 Choose an alternative font size from the list (use the scroll bar if necessary to bring the font size required into view)

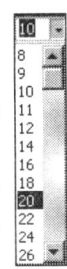

To change the font colour:
1 Select the cell (or cells)
2 Click the drop-down arrow to the right of the **Font Color** tool on the right-hand side of the Formatting toolbar
3 Click on the colour you want to use

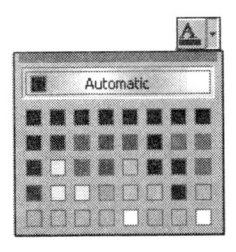

– 49 –

To change the background colour:

1 Select the cell (or cells)
2 Click the drop-down arrow to the right of the **Fill Color** tool
3 Click on the colour you want to use

To apply a border to a cell (or cells):

1 Select the cell (or cells)
2 Click the drop-down arrow to the right of the **Border** tool
3 Select the border effect you wish to use
4 Deselect your cell (or cells)

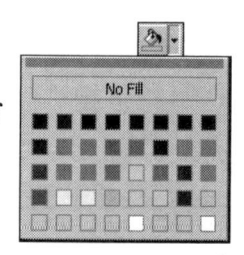

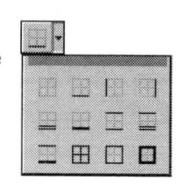

Format Cells dialog box

The formatting options can also be found in the Format Cells dialog box, on the Alignment, Font, Border and Patterns tabs.

To display the dialog box:

- Choose **Cells...** from the **Format** menu.

Experiment with the formatting options in your worksheets.

Headings for narrow columns can look better if set at an angle – drag the indicator in the Orientation box

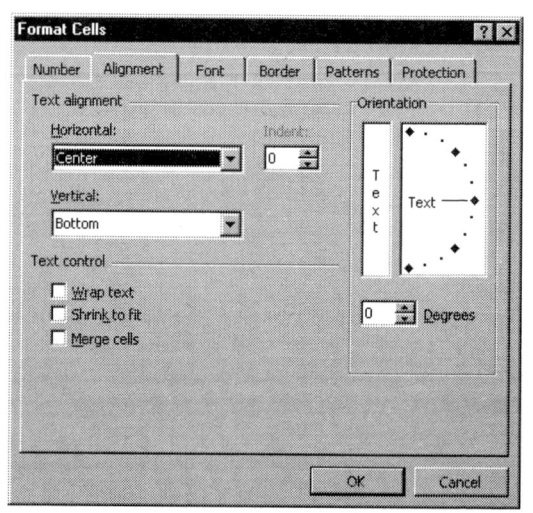

FORMATTING AND LAYOUT

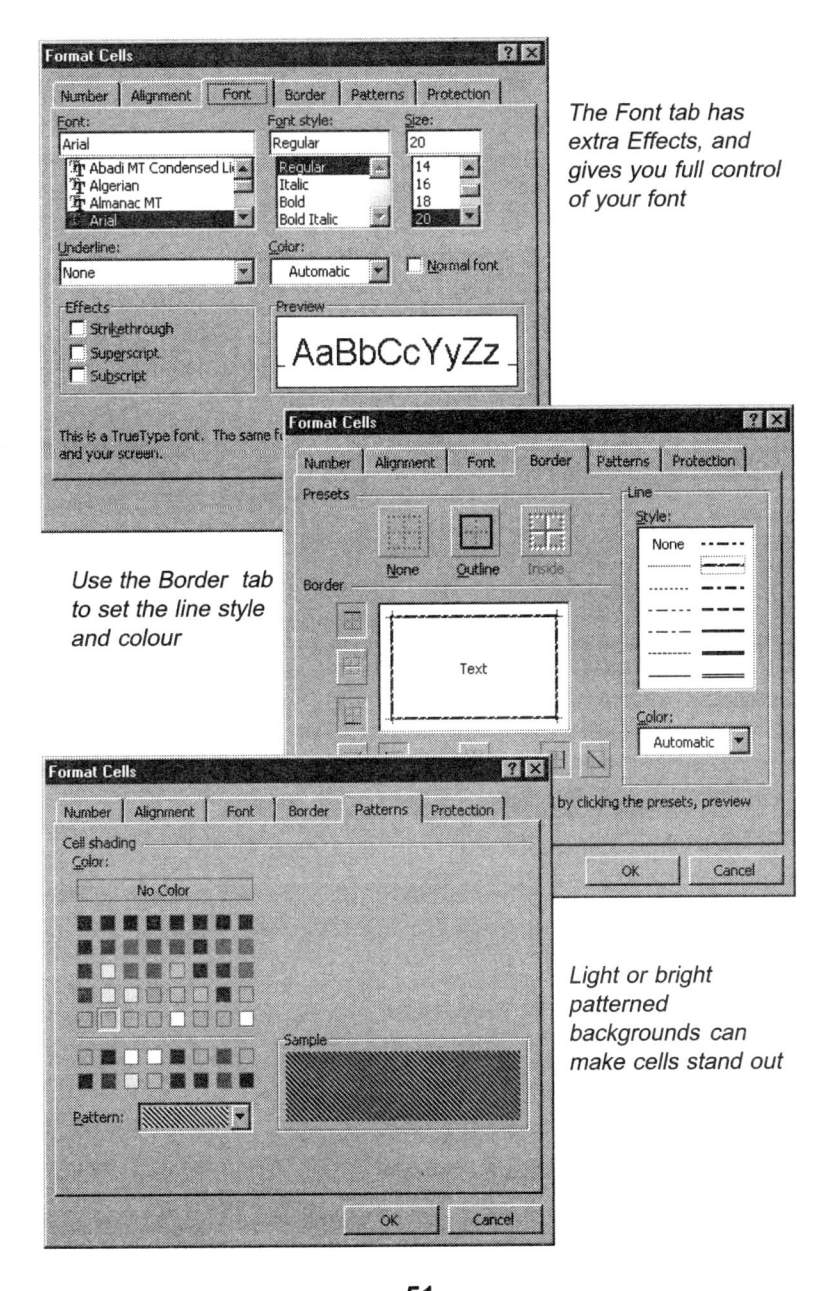

The Font tab has extra Effects, and gives you full control of your font

Use the Border tab to set the line style and colour

Light or bright patterned backgrounds can make cells stand out

3.5 Format Painter

If you have applied several formatting options to a cell, and you want to apply the same formatting to some other cells in your worksheet you could save yourself some time by using the Format Painter.

The Format Painter allows you to copy the formatting from one cell, and paint it onto other cells.

To copy a format to a single cell, or to adjacent cells:

1. Select the cell that is formatted the way you want
2. Click the **Format Painter** tool on the Standard toolbar
3. Click on the cell you want to apply the formatting to

Or

- Click and drag over the cells to which you want to apply the formatting.

To copy a format to non-adjacent cells:

1. Select the cell that is formatted the way you want
2. Double click the **Format Painter** tool on the Standard toolbar – this 'locks' the Format Painter tool on
3. Click on the cell you want to apply the formatting to

Or

- Click and drag over the cells you want to paint with the formatting.

4. Click the Format Painter tool again (or press **[Esc]** on your keyboard) to switch the Format Painter off when you've finished

3.6 Change the default font

If you don't want to use the default font of Arial, size 10, you can change it. After setting a new default, you must restart Excel before it takes effect. Every new workbook you create will use the font you have set as the default (until you change it again).

To change the default font:

1 Open the **Tools** menu and choose **Options**
2 Select the **General** tab
3 Set the **Standard font:** and **Size:** fields as required
4 Click **OK**

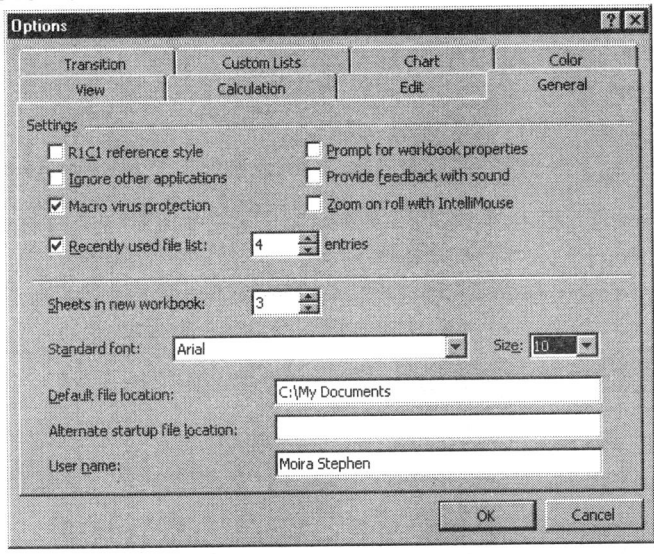

5 Click **OK** at the prompt that appears

6 Exit Excel and restart it again for the change to take effect

3.7 Freeze panes

Most of the worksheets you create will be considerably larger than will fit on to your computer screen. You will need to scroll vertically and horizontally to display the data you want to work with.

When you scroll your worksheet, the column headings or row labels will disappear off your screen as the other data appears. This is often very inconvenient, as you need to see the column headings or row labels to make sense of your data.

In a situation like this you should *freeze* part of your worksheet window so that it doesn't move, and scroll the part of your window that you haven't frozen.

To freeze a row (or rows):

1 Select the row below the ones you want to freeze

To freeze a column (or columns):

- Select the column to the right of the ones you want to freeze.

To freeze a both a row (or rows) and column (or columns):

- Select the cell below and to the right of where you want to freeze the panes.

Pane frozen at Row 5

	A	B	C	D	E	F
4						
5	Item	Code	Rec Retail Price	*Sale Price*	Saving	
8	Badminton Racket	B25	£24.00	**£15.66**	£8.34	
9	Squash Racket	S44-A	£27.75	**£19.99**	£7.76	
10	Hockey Stick	H220	£ 16.99	£ 9.99	£7.00	
11	Hockey Stick	H221	£ 18.99	£ 10.99	£8.00	
12	Tennis Racket	T101	£ 35.99	£ 24.99	£11.00	
13	Badminton Racket	B17	£ 18.99	£ 14.00	£4.99	
14	Rucksack	R10	£ 14.99	£ 9.99	£5.00	
15	Dumbell Set	D12	£ 36.99	£ 26.99	£10.00	
16	Home Gym	HG3	£ 245.99	£ 175.00	£70.99	
17	Rucksack	R14	£ 12.99	£ 7.50	£5.49	

2 Open the **Windows** menu

3 Choose **Freeze Panes**

When you scroll through your worksheet horizontally, the column or columns you have frozen remain in view. When you scroll through your worksheet vertically the row or rows you have frozen will remain in view when the other data scrolls.

To unfreeze panes:

1 Open the **Windows** menu

2 Choose **Unfreeze Panes**

3.8 Split screen

There will also be times when you want to compare the data on one part of your worksheet with that on another – but the data ranges that you want to compare are in separate areas of the worksheet.

When this happens, you should *split* your screen so that you can scroll each part independently, to bring the data you require into view.

Split box

If you look carefully at the top of the vertical scroll bar (above the up arrow), or to the right of the horizontal scroll bar (outside the right arrow), you will notice the *split box*. You must use the split boxes to split your screen.

To split your screen horizontally:

- Drag the split box at the top of the vertical scroll bar down to where you want your split to be

To split your screen vertically:

- Drag the split box at the right of the horizontal scroll bar along to where you want your split to be

When your screen is split, you can scroll each pane independently to view the data you want to see.

	A	D	E	F
4	Item	Sale Price	Saving	
5	Holdall (blue Nylon)	£ 9.99	£ 5.51	
6	Rucksack	£ 9.99	£ 7.00	
7	Badminton Racket	£ 15.66	£ 8.34	
8	Squash Racket	£ 19.99	£ 7.76	
9	Hockey Stick	£ 9.99	£ 7.00	
10	Hockey Stick	£ 10.99	£ 8.00	
11	Tennis Racket	£ 24.99	£ 11.00	
12	Badminton Racket	£ 14.00	£ 4.99	
13	Rucksack	£ 9.99	£ 5.00	
14	Dumbell Set	£ 26.99	£ 10.00	

Split box

To remove a split:

- Double click the split.

3.9 Page layout

In the previous chapter we discussed printing your worksheet. We will now consider some of the ways in which you can change the appearance (or layout) of your printed worksheet.

Orientation

Pages are usually printed *portrait* (▯ rather than *landscape* ▭).

To change the orientation:

1 From a worksheet, open the **File** menu and choose **Page Setup**

Or

- If you are in Print Preview, click the **Setup...** button on the Print Preview toolbar to open the **Page Setup** dialog box

2 Select the **Page** tab

3 Choose the **Orientation** option required – *Portrait* or *Landscape*

4 Click **OK**

Scaling

If your worksheet is more than a page in size, you can specify the number of pages you want the worksheet to be printed on by using the scaling option.

1 Open the **Page Setup** dialog box and select the **Page** tab

2 In the **Scaling** options, specify the number of pages wide and the number of pages tall you want your worksheet to fit on

3 Click **OK**

- This option is particularly useful if the last page of your worksheet contains only a small amount of data. You can specify that the worksheet print on one page less than it really needs – Excel will scale it down to fit on that number of pages.

Page size

The default paper size used for printing is A4. You can select an alternative page size if necessary.

1 Open the **Page Setup** dialog box and select the **Page** tab

2 Choose the size required from the **Paper size** list

3 Click **OK**

Margins

You can change the margin settings for your worksheet in either Page Setup or in Print Preview.

To change the margins in the Page Setup dialog box:

1 Open the **Page Setup** dialog box and select the **Margins** tab

2 Specify the margins you want to use

3 Click **OK**

To change the margins while in Print Preview:

1 Click the **Margins** button on the Print Preview toolbar

- The margins appear as dotted lines around your page.

2 Drag the margins to the position required

Page breaks

If your worksheet runs to more than one page, Excel will divide the worksheet into pages by inserting automatic page breaks. Exactly where the page breaks appear depends on the paper size, margin settings and scaling options you have set.

You can set your own horizontal and vertical page breaks.

To insert a horizontal page break:

1 Select the row *below* where you want the page break to be

2 Open the **Insert** menu and click **Page Break**

To insert a vertical page break:

1 Select the column to the *right* of where you want to insert the page break

2 Open the **Insert** menu and click **Page Break**

To move a page break:

1 Open the **View** menu and click **Page Break Preview**

2 Drag the page break to its new position

To insert a horizontal and vertical page break at once:

1 Select the cell immediately below and to the right of where you want to start a new page

2 Open the **Insert** menu and click **Page Break**

To remove a page break:

1 Open the **View** menu and click **Page Break Preview**

2 *Right* click on a cell below a horizontal page break

Or
- *Right* click on a cell to the right of the vertical page break.
3 Click **Remove Page Break** on the shortcut menu
4 Open the **View** menu and click **Normal** to return to your worksheet

Headers and footers

Headers and footers display information at the top or bottom of every page that prints out for your worksheet. They are useful for page numbers, your name, the date that the worksheet is printed, the worksheet name, the workbook name – or any other information that you would like to appear in them.

To add a header and/or footer to your pages:
1 Open the **Page Setup** dialog box
2 Select the **Header/Footer** tab
3 Choose a header or footer from the list of options available
4 Click **OK**

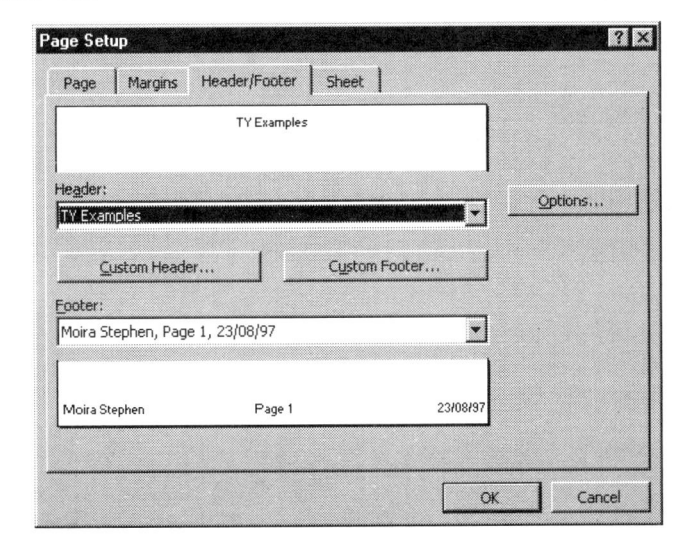

You don't need to use one of the options listed. You can set up any header or footer you want.

To set a custom Header or Footer:

1 Select the **Header/Footer** tab in the **Page Setup** dialog box

2 Click **Custom Header...** or **Custom Footer...**

3 Click in the section you want your header or footer to appear in – left, centre or right

4 Type in the text you want to appear in the header or footer

Or

- Click the appropriate button to add page numbers, date, time, file name or sheet name.

5 Click **OK**

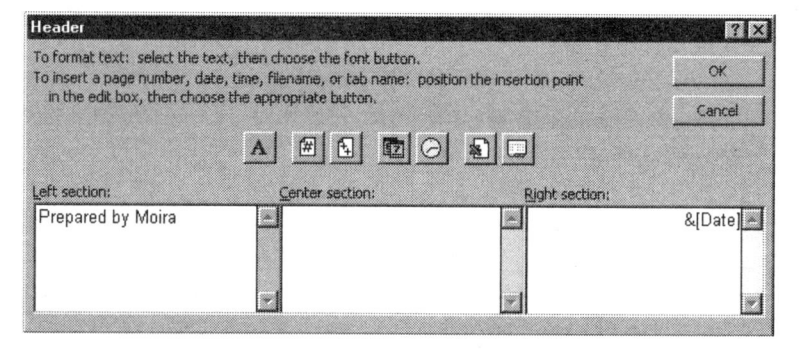

Gridlines, Row and Column Headings

When you print your worksheet out, the gridlines, row and column headings do not print. This is usually how you would want it, but there may be times when it is useful to print out the gridlines and/or the row and column headings – for example, when printing out the formulas and functions you have used (see Chapter 5).

You can specify that you want the gridlines, row and column headings to print in the Page Setup dialog box.

1 Open the **Page Setup** dialog box and select the **Sheet** tab

2 In the Print options, select the **Gridlines** and/or **Row and column headings** checkboxes as required

3 Click **OK**

Page order

If your worksheet is going to print out on more than one sheet of paper, the pages can be printed either **down then across** OR **across then down**. You can specify the order you prefer.

1 Open the **Page Setup** dialog box and select the **Sheet** tab

2 In the **Page order** options, select the order required

3 Click **OK**

3.10 Summary

This chapter has discussed some of the options available to help you format your worksheet. We've also looked at how you can freeze and split your screen and how you can modify the layout of your worksheet before you print it. We have considered:

- Bold, italic and underline.
- Alignment options – left, right, centre, centre across selection.
- Font, font size, font colour, background colour, cell borders.
- Format painter.
- Changing the default font.
- Keeping column and row labels displayed by freezing panes.
- Viewing different parts of a worksheet on the screen at the same time by splitting the screen.
- Page layout options – orientation, scaling, page size, margins, page breaks, headers and footers, gridlines, row and column headings and page order.

4

WORKING WITH SHEETS

4.1 Aims of this chapter

This chapter addresses some of the options you will find useful when working with worksheets. We will discuss some things you might like to consider when designing a worksheet. You will learn how to add worksheets to a workbook, delete them, rename them, copy them and move them. You will also find out how to group worksheets and enter data, text or formulas on several worksheets simultaneously.

4.2 Moving between worksheets

The worksheet tabs appear at the bottom left of your screen – to the left of the horizontal scrollbar.

To move from one sheet to another in your workbook:
- Click the sheet tab of the sheet you want to work on

If you can't see all the sheet tabs in the sheet tab bar, use the buttons to the left of the tabs to scroll the sheet tabs into view.

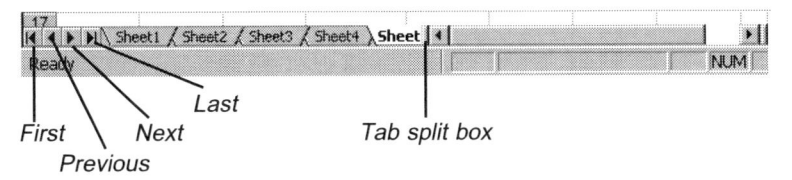

```
First    Next            Tab split box
         Last
         Previous
```

You can change the amount of space allocated to the sheet tab bar and the horizontal scroll bar by dragging the Tab split box between the sheet tabs and the horizontal scroll bar.

4.3 Worksheet design

Before you start setting up your worksheet, you should give some thought to the design of your worksheet.

The main areas to keep in mind:

1 Work out the purpose of your worksheet. Ask yourself:

- What do you want to communicate?

- What should be emphasised or de-emphasised?

- How should you indicate the relationship between areas on your worksheet?

2 Keep it simple.

3 Be consistent – within a worksheet and across worksheets. If you produce the same worksheet every month your regular reader will be able to find the information he or she needs quickly if it's always in the same place.

4 Use formatting and layout options to add contrast to different areas of your worksheet.

There are no hard and fast rules – the main objective is to display the data in a clear and unambiguous way. If you like the layout and your audience can understand it, it's probably okay.

Some Dos and Don'ts of worksheet design:

DO make sure you use a font that is easy to read – Arial (the default) is a very 'clean' font, Times New Roman is easy on the eye.

DO make use of 'white space' if you have room. This just means leave some blank rows or columns between sections of your worksheet to make it easier to read.

DO use borders and/or shading effects to divide large worksheets up into manageable chunks and to draw attention to subtotals and totals.

DO format your numbers appropriately – currency, number of decimal places, percentage, etc.

DO make sure your worksheet is legible – don't use too small a font size or shrink to fit data so that it is too small to read.

DO add comments to cells that need an explanation.

DON'T use too many different fonts or font sizes on a worksheet.

DON'T go overboard with font and fill colours – you'll give everyone a headache!

DON'T print gridlines out on final reports – they may be useful on a draft printout, or one with formula displayed, but they give a very cluttered look to a final report.

4.4 Adding worksheets

When you create a workbook in Excel 97 the default number of worksheets in the workbook is three. This may be enough (or more than enough) on some occasions. However, if you need more than three worksheets in your workbook you can easily add them.

To insert a worksheet:

1 Select the worksheet (click on the sheet tab) you want to have to the right of the new one

2 Open the **Insert** menu and choose **Worksheet**

Or

1 Right click on the worksheet tab you want to have to the right of the new one
2 Choose **Insert** from the shortcut menu
3 Select the **General** tab in the **Insert** dialog box
4 Choose **Worksheet** and click **OK**

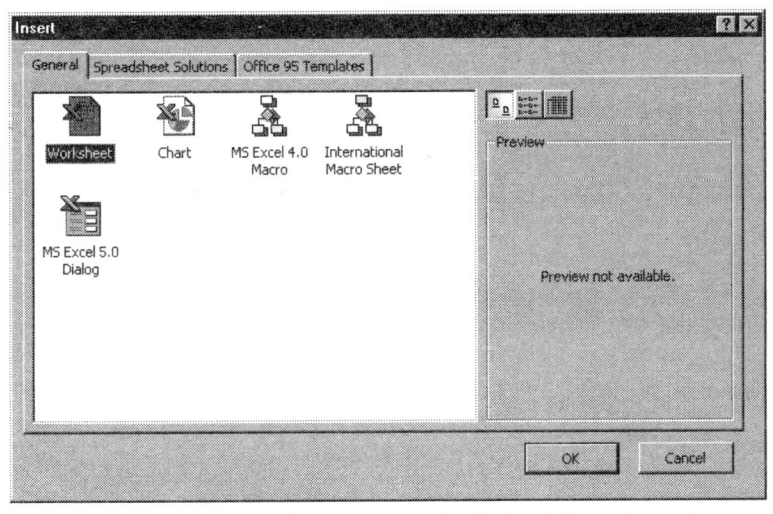

- A new worksheet will appear to the left of the selected one.

If you need to add new worksheets to most of your workbooks, you could change the default number of sheets in a new workbook to save you always having to add more.

To change the default number of sheets in a workbook:

1 Open the **Tools** menu and choose **Options**
2 Select the **General** tab
3 Set the number of sheets you require in the **Sheets in new workbook:** field
4 Click **OK**

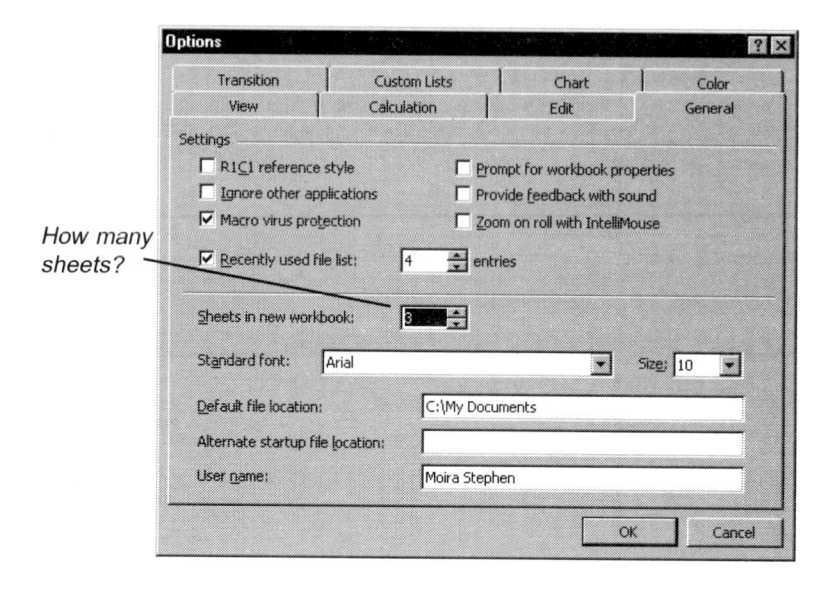

How many sheets? — (annotation pointing to "Sheets in new workbook" field in the Options dialog, General tab)

4.5 Deleting worksheets

If your workbook contains too many sheets you can easily delete any you don't need.

To delete a worksheet:

1 Select the sheet you want to delete

2 Open the **Edit** menu and choose **Delete Sheet**

Or

1 Right click on the sheet tab of the sheet you want to delete

2 Select **Delete** from the shortcut menu

3 Respond to the prompt – click **OK** if you really want to delete the sheet, **Cancel** if you change your mind

- Be careful when deleting worksheets – **Undo** will not restore them for you!

4.6 Renaming worksheets

By default, worksheets are named *Sheet1*, *Sheet2*, *Sheet3*, etc. If you only use one or two sheets in a workbook this may cause you no problems. However, if you have several worksheets, life would be a bit easier if you renamed the worksheets to give them a name that actually meant something.

To rename a worksheet:

1 Select the worksheet you want to rename

2 Open the **Format** menu, choose **Sheet** then **Rename**

3 The sheet tab name will become selected

4 Type in the name you want to use

5 Press **[Enter]** or click anywhere on the worksheet

Or

1 Double click on the sheet tab you want to rename

2 Type in the name you want to use

3 Press **[Enter]** or click anywhere on the worksheet

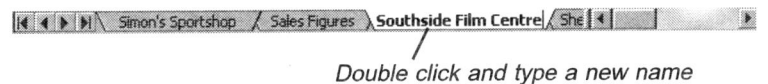

Double click and type a new name

4.7 Moving and copying worksheets

If you want to change the position of a worksheet within your workbook, you can move it to the position required. You can also move a worksheet to a different or new workbook.

To move a worksheet:

1 Select the worksheet you want to move or copy

2 Open the **Edit** menu and choose **Move** or **Copy Sheet...**

3 Choose the book you want to move or copy the worksheet to in the **To book**: field

– 67 –

4 Select a sheet – this doesn't apply if you choose *New book* in the **To Book** field.

5 Select **Create a copy** if you want to make a copy of the sheet rather than move it

6 Click **OK** – the sheet will be inserted before the one you selected.

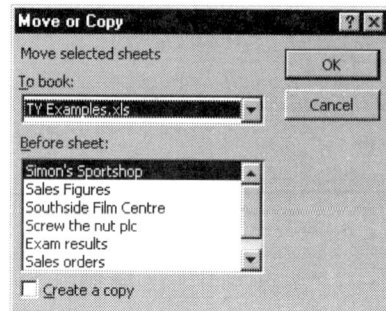

- If you move or copy your worksheet to a new book, remember to save the new workbook.

You can also move or copy worksheets within a workbook by dragging the worksheet to the position required.

To move the worksheet:

1 Click and drag the worksheet tab of the sheet you want to move along the sheet tabs until it is in the correct place

To copy the worksheet:

2 Hold the **[Ctrl]** key down while you click and drag the worksheet tab to the required position

4.8 Grouping worksheets

There may be times when you want to enter the same text, data or formulas into corresponding cells in more than one worksheet.

You could enter your work onto one worksheet, then copy it onto the others, or you could *group* the worksheets together and enter the standard material that will appear on them all.

When worksheets are grouped, anything you do on one worksheet is automatically entered onto every worksheet in the group.

To group adjacent worksheets:

1 Click on the sheet tab of the first sheet you want in the group

2   Hold the **[Shift]** key down and click on the last sheet tab you want in the group

To group non-adjacent worksheets:

1   Click on the sheet tab of the first sheet you want in the group

2   Hold the **[Ctrl]** key down and click on each sheet tab that you want in the group

When worksheets are grouped the word **[Group]** appears on the workbook Title Bar.

To ungroup worksheets:

1   Click on any worksheet tab that isn't part of the group

Or

1   Right click on one of the grouped worksheet tabs

2   Choose **Ungroup Sheets** from the pop-up menu

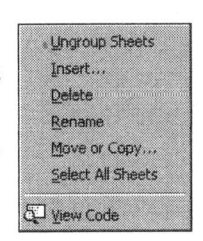

4.9 Summary

In this chapter we have discussed:

- Moving between sheets in a workbook.
- Things to consider when designing a worksheet layout.
- Adding sheets to a workbook.
- Changing the default number of sheets in a workbook.
- Deleting sheets from a workbook.
- Renaming sheets.
- Moving and copying sheets within a workbook.
- Moving and copying sheets to a new workbook.
- Grouping worksheets.

5

FORMULAS AND FUNCTIONS

5.1 Aims of this chapter

This chapter continues our discussion of formulas (introduced in Chapter 2) and introduces some of the many Excel functions that you might find useful. We will discuss AutoSum, statistical functions, named ranges, the IF function, cell comments and worksheet protection.

5.2 AutoSum

The worksheet below contains details of quarterly sales figures. Enter the text and data into a new worksheet in your workbook.

We need to calculate the total sales figure for each sales representative for the year and also the total sales figure for each quarter.

You could use a formula to calculate the total, e.g. **=B4+C4+D4+E4**, but the easiest and quickest way to calculate the total is to use AutoSum.

FORMULAS AND FUNCTIONS

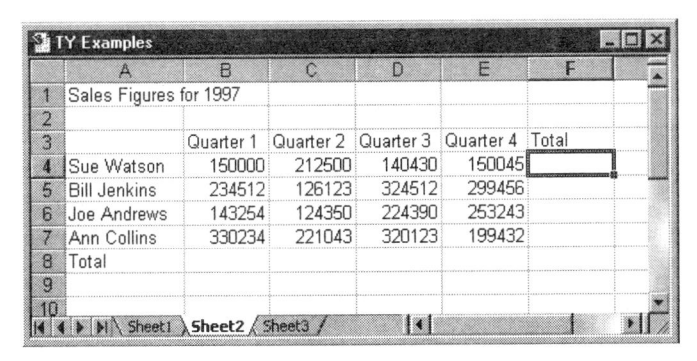

	A	B	C	D	E	F
1	Sales Figures for 1997					
2						
3		Quarter 1	Quarter 2	Quarter 3	Quarter 4	Total
4	Sue Watson	150000	212500	140430	150045	
5	Bill Jenkins	234512	126123	324512	299456	
6	Joe Andrews	143254	124350	224390	253243	
7	Ann Collins	330234	221043	320123	199432	
8	Total					

To calculate the totals using AutoSum:

1 Select a cell into which you want a total figure to appear, e.g. the cell that will contain the total sales for the first sales person or the total for Quarter 1

2 Click the **AutoSum** tool [Σ] on the Standard toolbar

3 The range of cells that are to be added will be highlighted. Note that the function appears in the Formula bar.

4 If the suggested range of cells is correct, press **[Enter]**

Or

- If the suggested range is not the range of cells you want to add together, drag over the correct range, then press **[Enter]**

The total value of the selected range of cells will appear in the active cell.

	A	B	C	D	E	F
						=SUM(B4:E4)
1	Sales Figures for 1997					
2						
3		Quarter 1	Quarter 2	Quarter 3	Quarter 4	Total
4	Sue Watson	150000	212500	140430	150045	=SUM(B4:E4)
5	Bill Jenkins	234512	126123	324512	299456	
6	Joe Andrews	143254	124350	224390	253243	
7	Ann Collins	330234	221043	320123	199432	
8	Total					

- Excel automatically calculates the total value of the selected cells using the **SUM** function. The syntax of this function is **=SUM (cell range)**. You could type in the function, but it's usually easier (and less error prone) to use AutoSum.

You could select the total cells in turn and use AutoSum to calculate the value that should appear in each, or use AutoFill (see 2.11) to copy the formula down or across the other total cells.

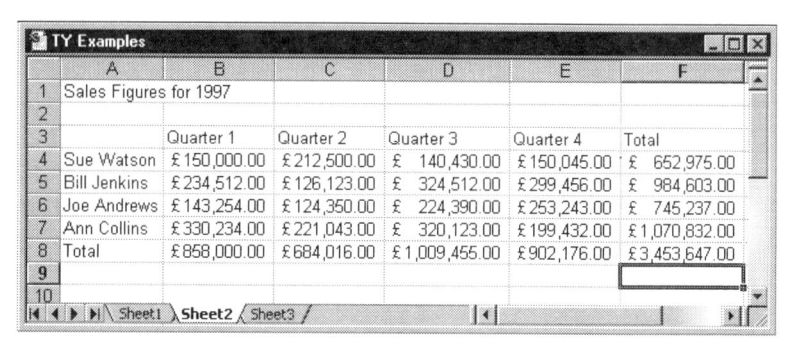

	A	B	C	D	E	F
1	Sales Figures for 1997					
2						
3		Quarter 1	Quarter 2	Quarter 3	Quarter 4	Total
4	Sue Watson	£150,000.00	£212,500.00	£ 140,430.00	£150,045.00	£ 652,975.00
5	Bill Jenkins	£234,512.00	£126,123.00	£ 324,512.00	£299,456.00	£ 984,603.00
6	Joe Andrews	£143,254.00	£124,350.00	£ 224,390.00	£253,243.00	£ 745,237.00
7	Ann Collins	£330,234.00	£221,043.00	£ 320,123.00	£199,432.00	£1,070,832.00
8	Total	£858,000.00	£684,016.00	£1,009,455.00	£902,176.00	£3,453,647.00

If you are totalling rows and columns, as in this example, you could use a shortcut to perform all the calculations in one move.

To AutoSum several groups of cells simultaneously:

1 Select all the rows and columns you want to total and the cells you want to contain the results of the AutoSum calculations

2 Click the **AutoSum** tool Σ on the Standard toolbar

The cells in the rightmost column and bottom row of the selected area will each have the Sum function inserted into them.

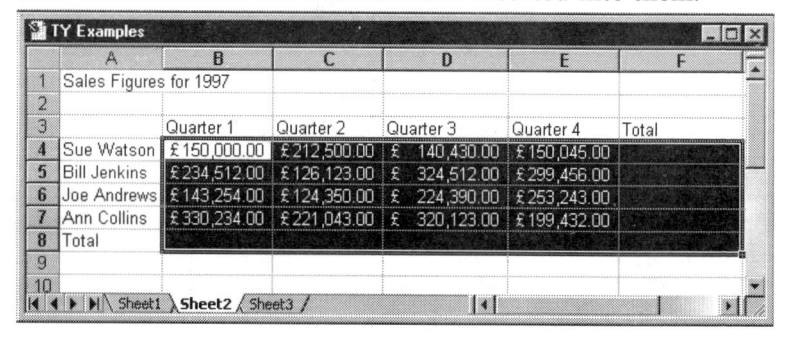

	A	B	C	D	E	F
1	Sales Figures for 1997					
2						
3		Quarter 1	Quarter 2	Quarter 3	Quarter 4	Total
4	Sue Watson	£150,000.00	£212,500.00	£ 140,430.00	£150,045.00	
5	Bill Jenkins	£234,512.00	£126,123.00	£ 324,512.00	£299,456.00	
6	Joe Andrews	£143,254.00	£124,350.00	£ 224,390.00	£253,243.00	
7	Ann Collins	£330,234.00	£221,043.00	£ 320,123.00	£199,432.00	
8	Total					

FORMULAS AND FUNCTIONS

Non-adjacent cells

You can also use AutoSum to total non-adjacent cells if you wish.

To total non-adjacent cells:

1 Select the cell that will contain the result of the calculation

2 Click the **AutoSum** tool on the Standard toolbar

3 Click on the first cell you want to include in the range of cells

4 Hold the **[Ctrl]** key down and click on each of the other cells to be included in the function

5 Press **[Enter]**

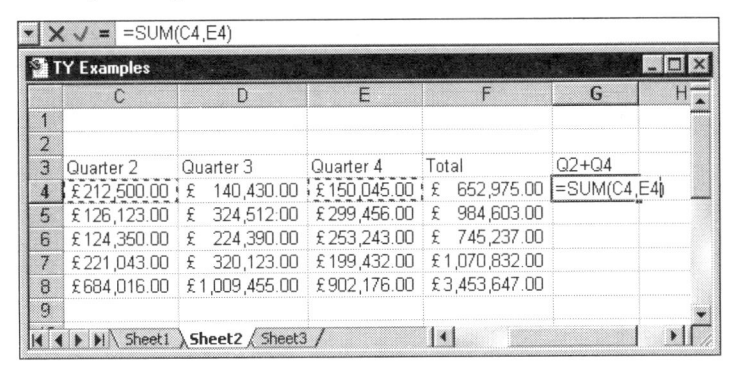

C	D	E	F	G
Quarter 2	Quarter 3	Quarter 4	Total	Q2+Q4
£212,500.00	£ 140,430.00	£150,045.00	£ 652,975.00	=SUM(C4,E4)
£126,123.00	£ 324,512.00	£299,456.00	£ 984,603.00	
£124,350.00	£ 224,390.00	£253,243.00	£ 745,237.00	
£221,043.00	£ 320,123.00	£199,432.00	£1,070,832.00	
£684,016.00	£1,009,455.00	£902,176.00	£3,453,647.00	

- If you prefer to type in the function, you must start with an **=** (equals sign). A range of adjacent cells have the first cell address in the range entered, followed by a **:** (colon), then the last cell address in the range. The cell addresses for non-adjacent cells must be separated by a **,** (comma).

5.3 Formula Palette

The Formula Palette is used to help you enter your formulas and functions. Before going on to enter more formulas and functions, have a look at the Formula Palette – it makes the generation of formulas and functions relatively easy!

– 73 –

- To display the Formula Palette, click the **Edit Formula** button (the = sign) to the left of the Formula bar.

The function currently being used is displayed at the top of the formula list, in the top left-hand corner of the palette.

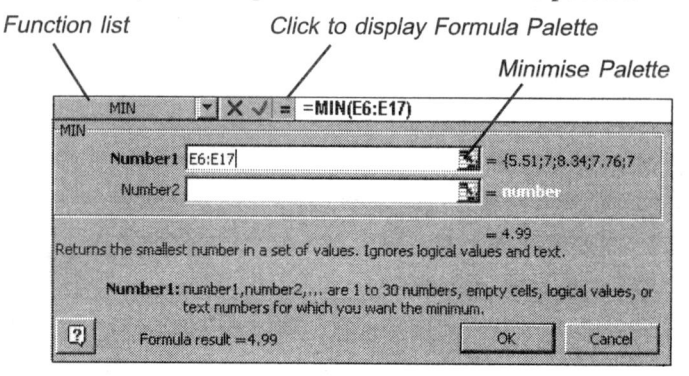

Function list   *Click to display Formula Palette*

Minimise Palette

- To change the function being used, click the drop-down arrow to display the function list, and select a different function.

- If the Formula Palette obscures the area of the worksheet you want to view, click the button to the right of a data entry field – the Formula Palette will become minimised, so you can see your worksheet.

Restore Palette

- To display the Palette again, click the restore Formula Palette button at the right-hand side of the minimised window.

5.4 Statistical functions

Statistical functions include minimum, maximum, average, count – and many others. The functions can be typed in through the keyboard, or you can use the Formula Palette, or the **Paste Function** command.

– 74 –

Minimum, Maximum, Average and Count

These can be used to display a value from a range of cells.

- To return the minimum value from a range use **MIN**.
- To return the maximum value from a range use **MAX**.
- To return the average value from a range use **AVERAGE**.
- To count the number of entries in a range use **COUNT**.

Using the Formula Palette:

1 Select the cell that the function will go in

2 Display the Formula Palette

3 Select the function from the function list, and jump to step 7

Or

4 If the function is not on the list, click **More Functions...** to display the **Paste Function** dialog box

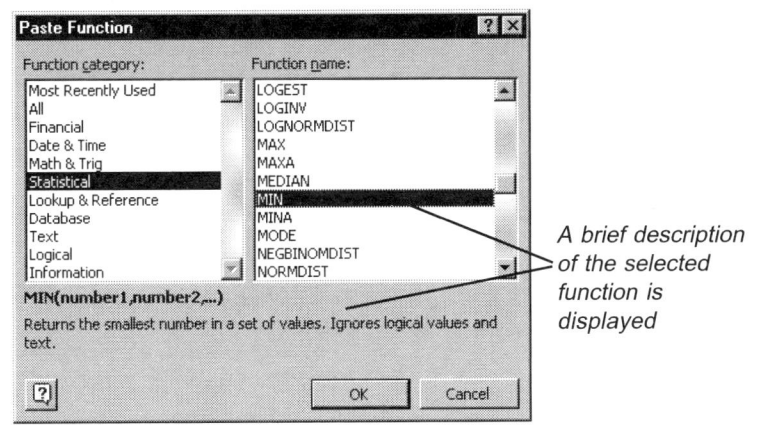

A brief description of the selected function is displayed

5 Select a category from the **Function category** list.

- If a function has been used recently, it will be listed in the *Most Recently Used* list. If you're not sure what category a function comes into, select the *All* category (every function is listed here, in alphabetical order). Minimum, Maximum, Average and Count can be found in the *Statistical* category.

6 Scroll through the **Function names** list, select the function you require and click **OK**

7 Enter the range of cells you want the function to operate on – either drag over the range on your worksheet, or enter the cell addresses through the keyboard (minimise the Formula Palette so that you can see your worksheet if necessary)

8 Restore the Formula Palette if necessary

9 Click **OK**

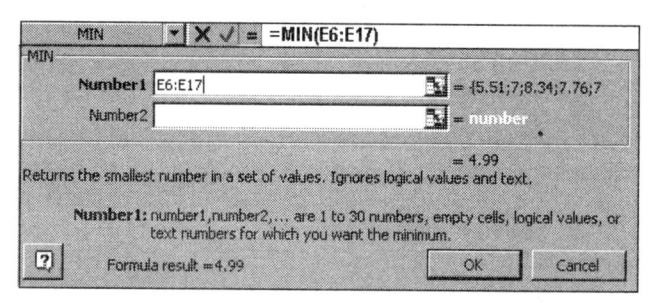

You can start from the Paste Function dialog box if you prefer, rather than from the Formula Palette. The methods are very similar.

Using Paste Function:

1 Select the cell that the function will go in

2 Click the **Paste Function** tool on the Standard toolbar

3 Select a category from the **Function category** list – *Most Recently Used* (if applicable), *All* or *Statistical*

4 Scroll through the **Function names** list, select the function required, then click **OK**

5 The Formula Palette will appear – specify the cells you want the function to work on

- Either drag over the range of cells you want to use in your workbook, or enter the cell range through the keyboard

6 Click **OK**

Return to your Simon's Sportshop worksheet (probably *Sheet1*, unless you've renamed it). Under the list of items for sale, enter functions to display:

- The minimum figure from the *Saving* column.
- The maximum figure from the *Saving* cloumn.
- The number of items in the sale.
- The average sale price of the items in the list.

	A	B	C
17			
18	Minumum Saving	£ 4.99	
19	Maximum Saving	£ 70.99	
20	Number of items in sale	12	
21	Average sale price	£ 27.92	
22			

5.5 View formula

When setting up your worksheet, it is sometimes useful to display and print the formulas and functions that you have entered into the cells.

Each formula or function is displayed in the Formula bar when its cell is selected, but you can get Excel to display all the formulas and functions in your worksheet if you wish.

To display the formulas and functions:

1 Open the **Tools** menu and select **Options...**
2 Select the **View** tab
3 Select the **Formulas** checkbox
4 Click **OK**

You may need to adjust the column widths to display the whole formula in some columns.

EXCEL 97

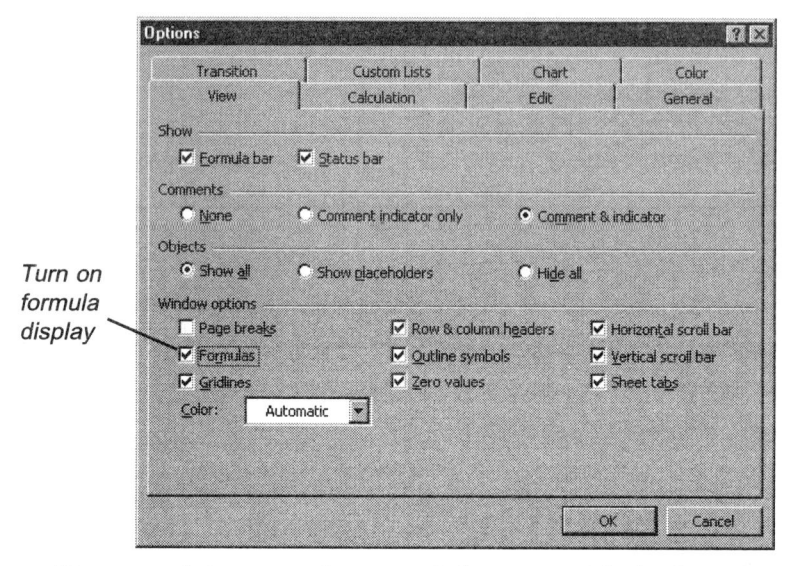

Turn on formula display — (pointing to Formulas checkbox in Options dialog, View tab)

- You can print a copy of your worksheet out with the formulas displayed – a printout is often useful for reference purposes.

The formulas and functions used in the Simon's Sportshop worksheet are displayed below.

```
                        Simon's Sportshop
            End of Season Sale - everything must go!
                                  Rec
                                  Retail    Sale
Item                  Code        Price     Price    Saving
Holdall (blue Nylon)  H123        15.5      9.99     =C6-D6
Rucksack              R12         16.99     9.99     =C7-D7
Badminton Racket      B25         24        15.66    =C8-D8
Squash Racket         S44-A       27.75     19.99    =C9-D9
Hockey Stick          H220        16.99     9.99     =C10-D10
Hockey Stick          H221        18.99     10.99    =C11-D11
Tennis Racket         T101        35.99     24.99    =C12-D12
Badminton Racket      B17         18.99     14       =C13-D13
Rucksack              R10         14.99     9.99     =C14-D14
Dumbell Set           D12         36.99     26.99    =C15-D15
Home Gym              HG3         245.99    175      =C16-D16
Rucksack              R14         12.99     7.5      =C17-D17

Minumum Saving        =MIN(E6:E17)
Maximum Saving        =MAX(E6:E17)
Number of items in sale =COUNT(D6:D17)
Average sale price    =AVERAGE(D6:D17)
```

– 78 –

FORMULAS AND FUNCTIONS

- To hide the formulas and functions again, go back to the **View** tab in the **Options** dialog box, de-select the **Formulas** checkbox and click **OK**.

—5.6 Relative and absolute addresses—

You have already noticed that when you AutoFill or copy a formula or function, the cell addresses used in the formula change automatically, relative to the position you copy them to.

By default, the cell addresses used are what are called *relative addresses*.

There will be times when you use a cell address in a formula or function, want to copy the formula or function down some rows or across some columns, but you don't want the cell address to change relative to its new position.

In the example below, we are going to calculate the income from admissions to a film centre.

- Enter the data onto a new worksheet in your workbook (see 4.4 if you need to add a new sheet). DO NOT complete the *Revenue* columns – we will enter formulas to calculate the figures in these columns.

	A	B	C	D	E	F	G
1	**SOUTHSIDE FILM CENTRE**						
2	MONTHLY TAKINGS FROM ADMISSIONS						
3							
4	Admission Charges						
5	Adult	£ 2.80					
6	OAP	£ 2.40					
7	Concession	£ 2.25					
8							
9		January		February		March	
10		Number	Revenue	Number	Revenue	Number	Revenue
11	Adult	2435		2367		2546	
12	OAP	1768		2431		2262	
13	Concession	3765		4350		4754	

To calculate the January revenue figures:

1 Enter a formula into the *Adult* cell in the *January, Revenue* column to calculate the income from this group. The first revenue figure for January is calculated by multiplying the number of adults visiting the film centre (B11) by the adult admission rate (B5). The formula in C11 should be **=B11*B5**.

2 Use AutoFill (see 2.11) to copy the formula down over the *OAP* and *Concession* cells

We could enter the appropriate formulas into the *February* and *March* columns in a similar way. However, it would be quicker to copy the *January* formulas, rather than enter them again.

This poses two possible problems:

- we don't want the B5 (Adult), B6 (OAP), B7 (Concession) cell addresses to change when we copy the formula across.

- we can't use AutoFill because the cells we want to copy to are not next to the source cells.

To stop the cell addresses changing when we copy them, we must create ***absolute addresses*** for them. An absolute address will not change when the formula or function it is in is copied or moved.

To create an absolute cell address:

- Enter a $ sign in front of each co-ordinate that you do not want to change.

You can type in the $ sign, or use the **[F4]** key on your keyboard.

To create absolute addresses for the cells in a formula:

1 Select the cell that contains the formula (C11 or C12 or C13 in this example) – the formula appears in the Formula bar

2 Click in the Formula bar

3 Place the insertion point to the right of the cell address you want to make absolute (B5 or B6 or B7)

4 Press the **[F4]** key until you have the cell addressed properly.

- Each time you press the **[F4]** key it moves through the

absolute addressing options.

B5 neither co-ordinate will change

B$5 the column will change if you copy the formula across columns

$B5 the row number will change if you copy the formula down rows

B5 both co-ordinates will change relative to its new position

Absolutely address the admission rate cell address in each of the *January* formula – either **B5** or **$B5** will do – we will eventually copy the formula across the columns, but must look back to column B for our data.

Once you've made absolute the cell addresses you don't want to change, you can copy the formula across to the *February* and *March* columns.

To complete the February and March figures:

1 Select the cells you are copying from – the *January* revenue figures in this case, C11:C13

2 Click the **Copy** tool on the Standard toolbar

3 Select the first cell you want to paste into, e.g. E11 for the *February* figures – you don't need to select E11:E13

4 Click the **Paste** tool on the Standard toolbar

5 Select cell G11 as the first cell for the *March* figures

6 Click the **Paste** tool on the Standard toolbar

7 Press **[Esc]** on your keyboard to cancel the copy routine

Your final worksheet should look similar to the one on the next page. The first picture displays the formulas (you may have different cell addresses if you have used different rows and columns for your data), the second one shows the results.

SOUTHSIDE FILM CENTRE
MONTHLY TAKINGS FROM ADMISSIONS

Admission Charges	
Adult	2.8
OAP	2.4
Concession	2.25

Showing formulas

	January		February		March	
	Number	Revenue	Number	Revenue	Number	Revenue
Adult	2435	=B11*B5	2367	=D11*B5	2546	=F11*B5
OAP	1768	=B12*B6	2431	=D12*B6	2262	=F12*B6
Concession	3765	=B13*B7	4350	=D13*B7	4754	=F13*B7

SOUTHSIDE FILM CENTRE
MONTHLY TAKINGS FROM ADMISSIONS

Admission Charges	
Adult	£ 2.80
OAP	£ 2.40
Concession	£ 2.25

Showing results

	January		February		March	
	Number	Revenue	Number	Revenue	Number	Revenue
Adult	2435 £	6,818.00	2367 £	6,627.60	2546 £	7,128.80
OAP	1768 £	4,243.20	2431 £	5,834.40	2262 £	5,428.80
Concession	3765 £	8,471.25	4350 £	9,787.50	4754 £	10,696.50

5.7 Circular references

If you create a formula that refers back to its own cell, you create a circular reference. Excel cannot resolve circular references using normal calculation methods and a warning message will appear should a circular reference occur.

If the circular reference is accidental, click **OK** – the **Circular Reference** toolbar will appear and tracer arrows (blue dots when they point from a cell that provides data to another cell, and red dots if a cell contains an error value, e.g. #VALUE!)

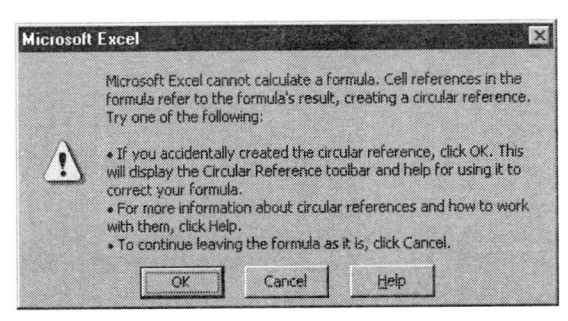

FORMULAS AND FUNCTIONS

Microsoft Excel

Microsoft Excel cannot calculate a formula. Cell references in the formula refer to the formula's result, creating a circular reference. Try one of the following:

- If you accidentally created the circular reference, click OK. This will display the Circular Reference toolbar and help for using it to correct your formula.
- For more information about circular references and how to work with them, click Help.
- To continue leaving the formula as it is, click Cancel.

[OK]   [Cancel]   [Help]

You can use the Circular Reference toolbar to move through each reference and redesign the formula so it doesn't cause a problem.

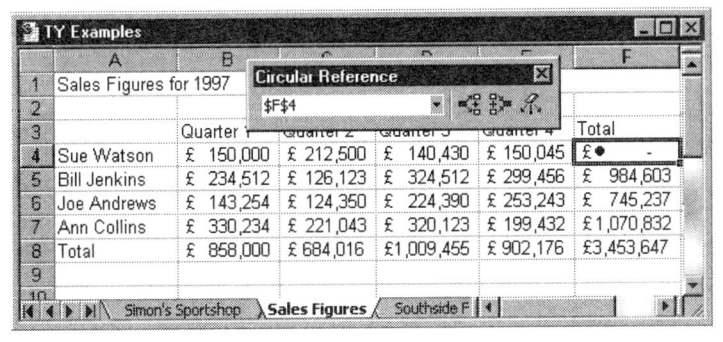

	A	B	C	D	E	F
1	Sales Figures for 1997		Circular Reference F4			
2						
3		Quarter 1	Quarter 2	Quarter 3	Quarter 4	Total
4	Sue Watson	£ 150,000	£ 212,500	£ 140,430	£ 150,045	£ -
5	Bill Jenkins	£ 234,512	£ 126,123	£ 324,512	£ 299,456	£ 984,603
6	Joe Andrews	£ 143,254	£ 124,350	£ 224,390	£ 253,243	£ 745,237
7	Ann Collins	£ 330,234	£ 221,043	£ 320,123	£ 199,432	£1,070,832
8	Total	£ 858,000	£ 684,016	£1,009,455	£ 902,176	£3,453,647

Simon's Sportshop \ **Sales Figures** / Southside F

To redesign the formula:

1 Select the cell that is causing a problem

2 Edit the formula in the Formula bar

- When the circular reference problem is resolved, the Circular Reference toolbar will disappear.

Some engineering and scientific formulas require circular references – in this case you may need to change the number of *iterations* (the number of times Excel recalculates the worksheet).

To change the number of iterations:

1 Choose **Options** from the **Tools** menu

2 On the **Calculation** tab, select the **Iteration** checkbox then specify the maximum number of iterations and degree of change you want Excel to use

5.8 Named ranges

When building up your formulas and functions, you have been using cell addresses to tell Excel which cells you want to use in your calculations. Cell addresses are not really very 'user friendly' – it isn't always immediately clear what the formula **=B13*B6** or the function **=AVERAGE(D5:D17)** is actually doing.

To make your worksheet easier to understand you can use named ranges instead of cell addresses in your formulas and functions.

There are two main ways of naming ranges.

- Use the row or column labels to refer to the related data – Excel 97 refers to these as *Natural-language formulas*.

Or

- Create descriptive names that are not already used as labels.

Natural-language formulas

In the example below, two versions of the same worksheet are illustrated, the top version is using the column and row labels in the function, and the lower one is using cell addresses.

```
Sales Figures for 1997

            Quarter 1       Quarter 2       Quarter 3       Quarter 4       Total
Sue Watson  150000          212500          140430          150045          =SUM(Sue Watson)
Bill Jenkins 234512         126123          324512          299456          =SUM(Bill Jenkins)
Joe Andrews 143254          124350          224390          253243          =SUM(Joe Andrews)
Ann Collins 330234          221043          320123          199432          =SUM(Ann Collins)
Total       =SUM(Quarter 1) =SUM(Quarter 2) =SUM(Quarter 3) =SUM(Quarter 4) =SUM(Total)


Sales Figures for 1997

            Quarter 1       Quarter 2       Quarter 3       Quarter 4       Total
Sue Watson  150000          212500          140430          150045          =SUM(B17:E17)
Bill Jenkins 234512         126123          324512          299456          =SUM(B18:E18)
Joe Andrews 143254          124350          224390          253243          =SUM(B19:E19)
Ann Collins 330234          221043          320123          199432          =SUM(B20:E20)
Total       =SUM(B17:B20)   =SUM(C17:C20)   =SUM(D17:D20)   =SUM(E17:E20)   =SUM(F17:F20)
```

I think you'll agree that the top version, using natural-language formulas, is easier to interpret than the lower one.

To create a formula using natural-language formulas:

- Type the row or column label into your formula in place of the cell or range you would have identified using addresses.

You can easily experiment with natural-language formulas. Delete the original formulas from the *Sales Figures* and/or the *Simon's Sportshop* worksheet in your workbook and type in natural-language formulas instead.

The *Simon's Sportshop* worksheet with natural-language formulas is shown below.

```
                        Simon's Sportshop
                  End of Season Sale - everything must go!

                         Rec Retail  Sale
Item                Code    Price    Price   Saving
Holdall (blue Nylon) H123   15.5     9.99    =Rec Retail Price - Sale Price
Rucksack            R12     16.99    9.99    =Rec Retail Price - Sale Price
Badminton Racket    B25     24       15.66   =Rec Retail Price - Sale Price
Squash Racket       S44-A   27.75    19.99   =Rec Retail Price - Sale Price
Hockey Stick        H220    16.99    9.99    =Rec Retail Price - Sale Price
Hockey Stick        H221    18.99    10.99   =Rec Retail Price - Sale Price
Tennis Racket       T101    35.99    24.99   =Rec Retail Price - Sale Price
Badminton Racket    B17     18.99    14      =Rec Retail Price - Sale Price
Rucksack            R10     14.99    9.99    =Rec Retail Price - Sale Price
Dumbell Set         D12     36.99    26.99   =Rec Retail Price - Sale Price
Home Gym            HG3     245.99   175     =Rec Retail Price - Sale Price
Rucksack            R14     12.99    7.5     =Rec Retail Price - Sale Price

Minumum Saving       =MIN(Saving)
Maximum Saving       =MAX(Saving)
Number of items in  :=COUNT(Sale Price)
Average sale price   =AVERAGE(Sale Price)
```

- The range names used in natural-language formulas apply to the cells in the current worksheet only – you can't use them to access a range of cells in a formula from another worksheet.

Create named ranges

If your data does not have column or row labels, or if you want to use information that is stored on another sheet within the same workbook, you can create a name that describes the cell or cells.

Named ranges that you create are available to any worksheet within the workbook.

Rules for naming ranges

- The maximum size for a name is 255 characters.

- Spaces are not allowed (use an underline character or a full stop instead).

- The first character in a name must be a letter or an underline character (other characters can be letters, numbers, full stops and underline characters).

- You cannot use a cell reference for a name, e.g. B75 or AA$24.

- Names can contain upper and lower case letters. Excel is not case sensitive. If you create a name called *Profit*, then another range called *PROFIT*, the second name will replace the first.

To name a cell, or range of cells, within a worksheet:

1 Select the cell or range of cells you want to name

2 Click the **Name** box at the left edge of the Formula bar

3 Type in a name for the cells

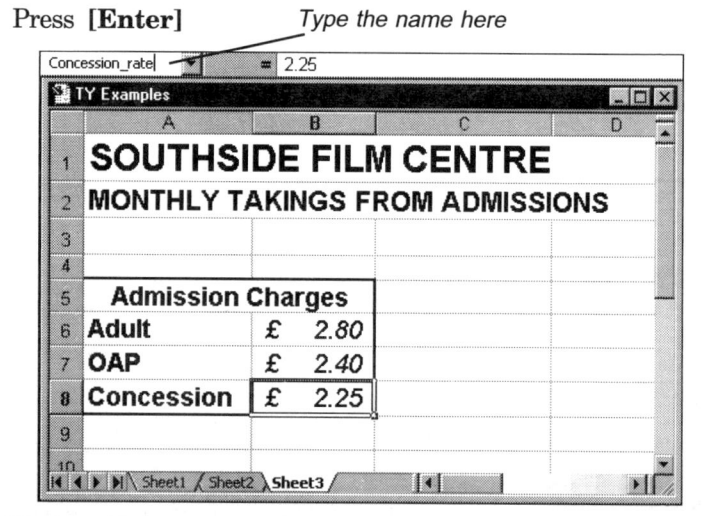

4 Press **[Enter]**

- You could create naming ranges for the admission charges in the Film Centre worksheet. You could name the cells *Adult_rate*, *OAP_rate* and *Concession_rate*.

To name cells using the existing row and column headings:

1 Select the cells you want to name – including the row and/or column headings

2 Open the **Insert** menu and choose **Name**, then **Create**

3 In the **Create Names** dialog box, select the location that contains the labels by selecting the appropriate checkbox(es)

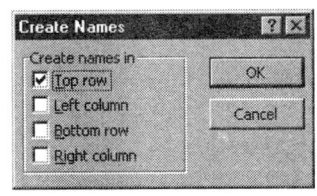

4 Click **OK**

- You could create named ranges for the columns in the *Screw the nut plc* worksheet using this method.

In the examples so far, the named ranges that have been created have represented a cell or group of cells on one worksheet. You can also create a named range for a group of cells taken from different worksheets in your workbook. It doesn't matter which sheet is active when you start this process, as you identify the worksheets you want to refer to in the **Define Name** dialog box.

1 Open the **Insert** menu and choose **Name**, then **Define**

2 Enter a name into the **Names in workbook** field

3 Delete any data that appears in the **Refers to** field

4 Type an = sign into the **Refers to** field

5 Click the tab for the first worksheet to be included

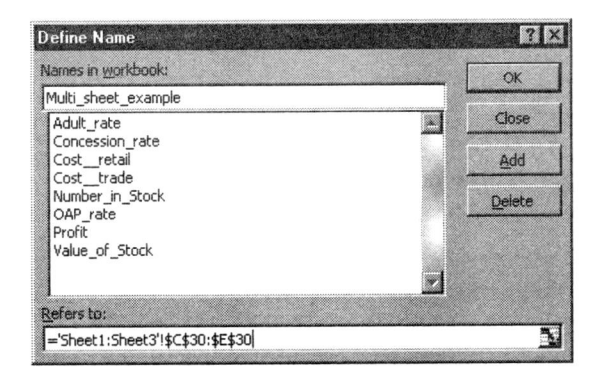

6 Hold the **[Shift]** key down and click the tab for the last worksheet to be included

7 Select the cell or range of cells to be named

8 Click **Add**

9 Click **OK** when you've finished

- In this example, the name *Multi_sheet_example* has been applied to the range C30:E30 on Sheet1, Sheet2 and Sheet3.

If you no longer use a range name, you can delete it. Deleting the range name does not delete the cell contents.

To delete a range name:

1 Open the **Insert** menu and choose **Name**, then **Define**

2 Select the range name you want to delete

3 Click **Delete** and close the **Define Name** dialog box

You can easily paste range names into your formula or function, rather than use the cell addresses.

To use a range name in a formula or function:

1 Select the cell that will contain the formula

2 Enter the formula as normal until you want to refer to a range

3 Open the **Insert** menu, choose **Name** then **Paste**

4 Select the name, then click **OK**

5 Continue building up your formula

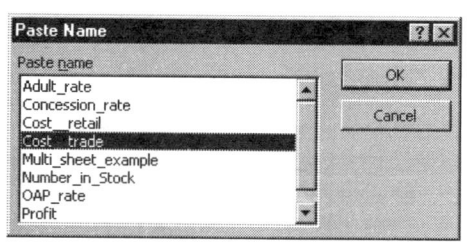

CONVERTING CELL ADDRESSES TO NAMED RANGES

If you have already set up formulas in your worksheet using cell addresses, and have then gone on to create names for some of the cells and ranges, you can easily convert the formulas to use the range names instead of the cell addresses.

1   If you want to convert all of the cell addresses to named ranges, select any single cell in your worksheet

Or

- If you want to convert only part of a sheet, select the range

2   Open the **Insert** menu, choose **Name** then **Apply**
3   Select the names from the **Apply names** list
4   Click **OK**

- If you have named ranges for the columns in the *Screw the nut plc* worksheet, try converting the formulas using this method.

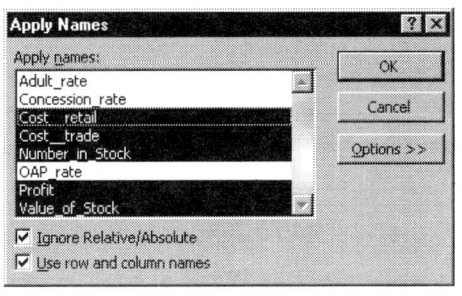

- The cell addresses in formulas that have range names will have the range names applied to the formulas and functions.

The *Screw the nut plc* worksheet is displayed below. The cell addresses originally used in the formulas were converted to the named ranges using the method described above.

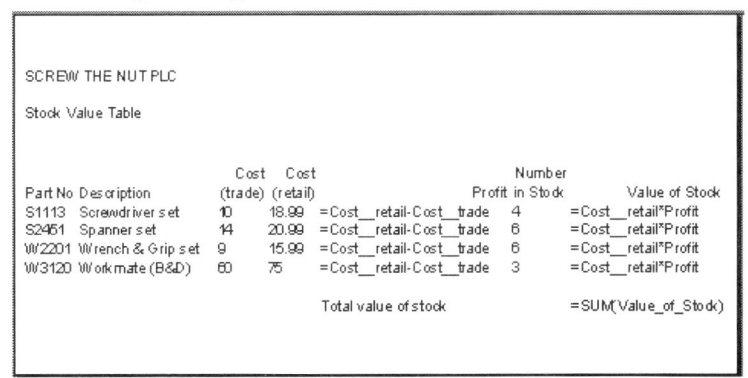

```
SCREW THE NUT PLC

Stock Value Table

                         Cost   Cost                              Number
Part No  Description    (trade) (retail)                        Profit in Stock      Value of Stock
S1113    Screwdriver set    10   18.99   =Cost__retail-Cost__trade    4       =Cost__retail*Profit
S2451    Spanner set        14   20.99   =Cost__retail-Cost__trade    6       =Cost__retail*Profit
W2201    Wrench & Grip set   9   15.99   =Cost__retail-Cost__trade    6       =Cost__retail*Profit
W3120    Workmate (B&D)     60   75      =Cost__retail-Cost__trade    3       =Cost__retail*Profit

                                         Total value of stock              =SUM(Value_of_Stock)
```

5.9 IF function

The IF function is used to return one value if a condition is True, and another value if the condition is False. The values returned can be text, numbers, or the result of a formula or function.

For example, you might be entering end-of-term exam results into a worksheet. If a student has 50% or more in the exam, a pass is awarded, if less than 50% is achieved, the result is a fail.

Comparison operators

This example uses a comparison operator to check if the Total Mark is greater than or equal to 50. The operators include:

- = equal to
- <> not equal to
- > greater than
- >= greater than or equal to
- < less than
- <= less than or equal to

Enter the data below into a new worksheet:

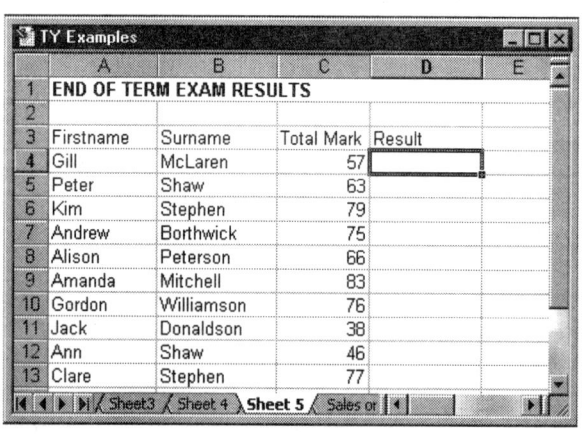

	A	B	C	D
1	END OF TERM EXAM RESULTS			
2				
3	Firstname	Surname	Total Mark	Result
4	Gill	McLaren	57	
5	Peter	Shaw	63	
6	Kim	Stephen	79	
7	Andrew	Borthwick	75	
8	Alison	Peterson	66	
9	Amanda	Mitchell	83	
10	Gordon	Williamson	76	
11	Jack	Donaldson	38	
12	Ann	Shaw	46	
13	Clare	Stephen	77	

To return a Pass or Fail message in the Result column, we need to enter the IF function.

To enter the function:

1 Select the first cell in the result column

2 Click the **Edit Formula** button (the **=** sign) to the left of the Formula bar

3 Select the **IF** function from the list (if it isn't listed go for **More functions** – you'll find it in the *All* or *Logical* category)

4 Enter the condition that you want to be evaluated in the **Logical _test** field (*Total Mark>=50* in this case)

5 Specify the value if the condition is true. Don't type the quotes – Excel will enter them automatically when you enter text

6 Specify the value if the condition is found to be false

7 Click **OK**

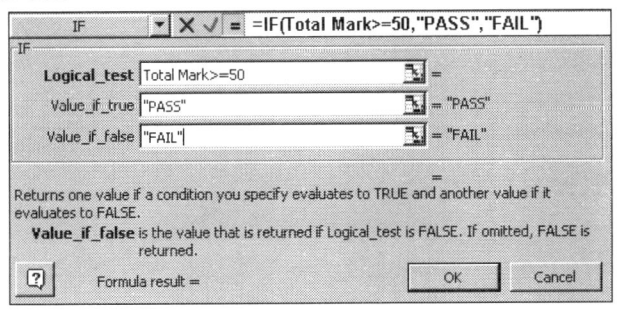

- AutoFill the function down through the *Result* column – *Pass* will appear in the rows where the condition is true, *Fail* will appear in the rows where the condition is false.

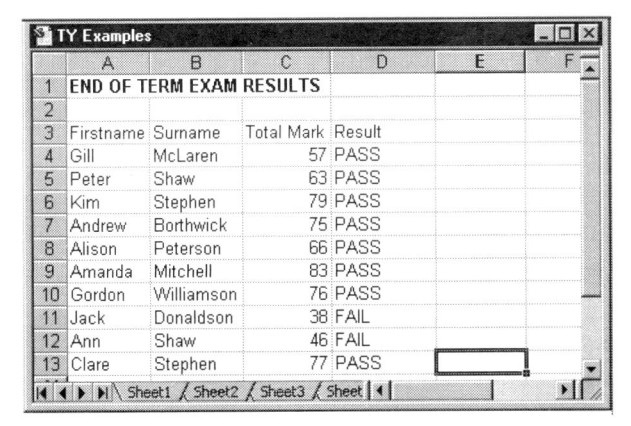

With the formulas displayed, the worksheet looks like the illustration below. This example uses natural-language rather than cell addresses. If we had used cell addresses the function would have been **=IF(C4>=50, "PASS", "FAIL")**

	A	B	C	D
1	END OF TERM EXAM RESULTS			
2				
3	Firstname	Surname	Total Mark	Result
4	Gill	McLaren	57	=IF(Total Mark>=50,"PASS","FAIL")
5	Peter	Shaw	63	=IF(Total Mark>=50,"PASS","FAIL")
6	Kim	Stephen	79	=IF(Total Mark>=50,"PASS","FAIL")
7	Andrew	Borthwick	75	=IF(Total Mark>=50,"PASS","FAIL")
8	Alison	Peterson	66	=IF(Total Mark>=50,"PASS","FAIL")
9	Amanda	Mitchell	83	=IF(Total Mark>=50,"PASS","FAIL")
10	Gordon	Williamson	76	=IF(Total Mark>=50,"PASS","FAIL")
11	Jack	Donaldson	38	=IF(Total Mark>=50,"PASS","FAIL")
12	Ann	Shaw	46	=IF(Total Mark>=50,"PASS","FAIL")
13	Clare	Stephen	77	=IF(Total Mark>=50,"PASS","FAIL")

Nested IFs

The values used by functions to perform calculations or operations are called *arguments*. An argument may be a numeric value, a text value, a cell reference, a range of cells, a named range, or a nested function (a function within a function).

This next example illustrates the use of a nested function. We are going to add another column to our worksheet to give the Grade achieved by each student. We need to use the IF function to check the Total Mark and return the appropriate grade.

- IF a student gets 70% or more, the grade is an A.
- IF the student gets between 60% and 69%, the grade is a B.
- IF the student gets between 50% and 59%, the grade is a C.
- Less than 50% is a fail.

As we have four possible outcomes this time (rather than a simple Pass or Fail) we must nest our IF functions to work through the various options.

- Add a new column heading – *Grade* – in the column to the right of the *Result* column.

1. Select the first cell in the *Grade* column
2. Click the **Edit Formula** button (the = sign) and select the IF function from the list
3. Enter the condition to be evaluated in the **Logical _test** field (*Total Mark>=70* in this case) and specify the **Value if true** – *A* (70% and over gets an A grade)
4. In the **Value if false** field, select **IF** again – we need to check if a student has 60% or more (this test will only be applied to students who did not get 70% or more)
5. Complete the next set of conditions and values. Enter the condition in the **Logical _test** field (*Total Mark>=60*) and specify the **Value if true** – *B* (60% – 69% gets a B grade).
6. In the **Value if false** field select **IF** again – we need to check if the student has 50% or more (this text will only be applied to students who did not get 60 – 69%)
7. Enter the **Logical _test** field (*Total Mark >=50* in this case)
8. Specify the **Value if true** – *C* (50% – 59% gets a C grade) and the **Value if false** – *Fail*
9. Click **OK**

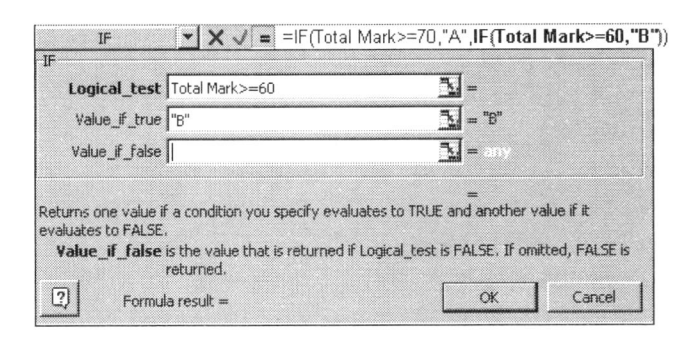

- AutoFill the functions down the column.

EXCEL 97

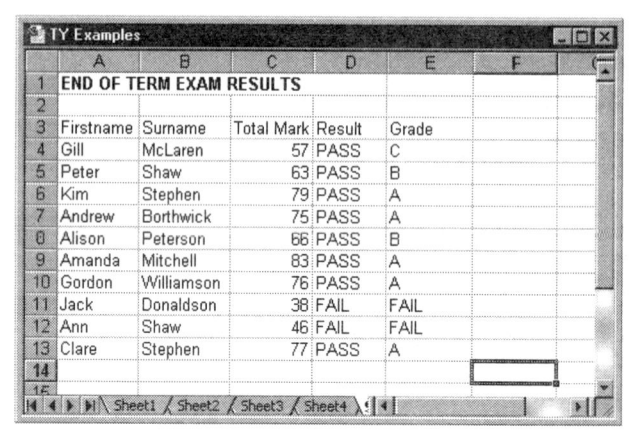

	A	B	C	D	E	F
1	END OF TERM EXAM RESULTS					
2						
3	Firstname	Surname	Total Mark	Result	Grade	
4	Gill	McLaren	57	PASS	C	
5	Peter	Shaw	63	PASS	B	
6	Kim	Stephen	79	PASS	A	
7	Andrew	Borthwick	75	PASS	A	
8	Alison	Peterson	66	PASS	B	
9	Amanda	Mitchell	83	PASS	A	
10	Gordon	Williamson	76	PASS	A	
11	Jack	Donaldson	38	FAIL	FAIL	
12	Ann	Shaw	46	FAIL	FAIL	
13	Clare	Stephen	77	PASS	A	

You should get A, B, C and Fail grades as appropriate. If you don't get the function to work as expected, delete it and try again.

In this next example, the IF function is used to work out the amount of discount a customer will get on an order.

- If the order is over £1000, a 10% discount will be deducted.
- If the value is between £750 and £999, a 5% discount is given.
- If the value of the order is less than £750, no discount is given.

Enter the basic worksheet as it is displayed below. The empty columns will be completed using functions and formulas.

	A	B	C	D	E	F
1	Sales Orders					
2						
3	Customer Code	Value of order	Discount	Net Amount	VAT	Total
4	ABC1	£ 1,523.75				
5	DEF2	£ 890.00				
6	GHI3	£ 600.00				

Named ranges have been created for the columns. These names have been created using the **Names**, **Define** option.

Natural language names do not work in the **Value if true**, **Value if false** fields in an IF function.

- The *Value of order* column has been called *VOO*.
- The *Discount* column has been called *Discount*.
- The *Net Amount* column has been called *Net_Amount*.
- The *VAT* column has been called *VAT*.

These names have been used in the functions and formulas. The formulas and functions required are displayed below.

```
Sales Orders

Customer Code   Value of order      Discount
ABC1            1523.75             =IF(VOO>=1000,VOO*10%,IF(VOO>=750,VOO*5%,0))
DEF2            890                 =IF(VOO>=1000,VOO*10%,IF(VOO>=750,VOO*5%,0))
GHI3            600                 =IF(VOO>=1000,VOO*10%,IF(VOO>=750,VOO*5%,0))


Net Amount       VAT                  Total
=VOO-Discount    =Net_Amount*17.5%    =Net_Amount+VAT
=VOO-Discount    =Net_Amount*17.5%    =Net_Amount+VAT
=VOO-Discount    =Net_Amount*17.5%    =Net_Amount+VAT
```

The other logical functions are AND, FALSE, NOT, OR and TRUE. Check them out in the on-line Help.

5.10 Comments

If you think that the purpose of a formula or function is not self-explicit, you can add a comment to the cell. Comments are particularly useful if you don't use named ranges, and want to add an explanation to a cell, or if others share your worksheets and you want to explain the logic behind an entry you have made.

To add a comment to a cell:

1 Select the cell you want to add a comment to
2 Open the **Insert** menu and choose **Comment**

3 Type your comment into the box

4 Click outside the comment box

If the comment remains on your screen, I suggest you change the comment view options to show the comment indicator only.

1 Open the **Tools** menu and choose **Options**

2 Select the **View** tab

3 In the **Comments** options, select the **Comment indicator only** radio button

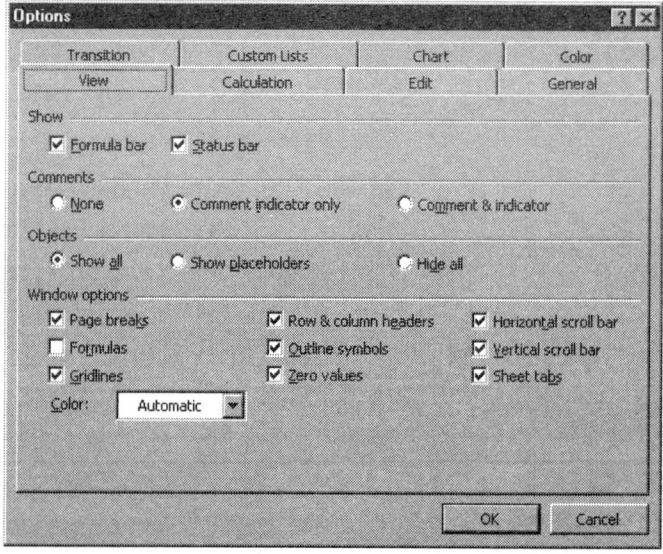

A small red triangle will appear in the top right corner of your cell to indicate that it has a comment attached to it.

When you move your mouse pointer over the cell, the comment will be displayed.

C	D	E
Discount	Net Amount	VAT
£152.38	Moira Stephen: 10% for orders over 1000	239.99
£ 44.50	5% for order between 750 and 1000	147.96
£ -	Less than that - no discount	105.00

FORMULAS AND FUNCTIONS

5.11 Cell protection

Having gone to the trouble of setting up formulas and functions on your worksheet, it would be a pity if they were accidentally overwritten when you are entering text and data.

You can protect the cells that you don't want to change to avoid this unfortunate situation arising.

Cell protection is a two-stage process in Excel. First, you must identify the cells you don't want protected, then you must protect your worksheet.

Once the worksheet has been protected, only those cells that you identified as the ones not to be protected can by modified (unless you 'unprotect' the worksheet again).

To identify the cells that are not to be protected:

1 Select the cells (you may have to do this in several stages)
2 Open the **Format** menu and choose **Cells...**
3 Select the **Protection** tab
4 De-select the **Locked** checkbox

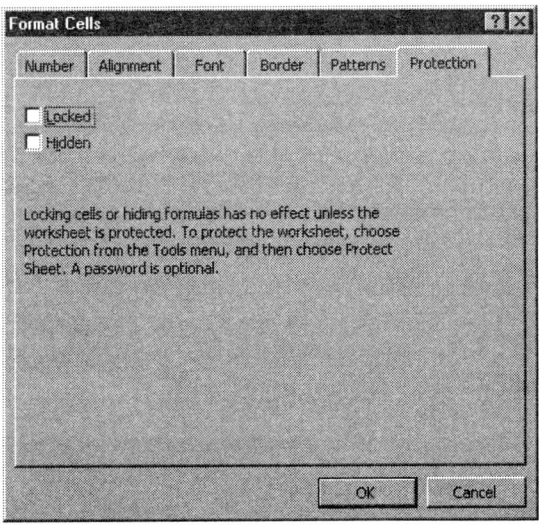

To activate the protection:

1 Open the **Tools** menu and choose **Protection**

2 Select **Protect Sheet** (or whatever option is appropriate)

3 Set a **Password** if you wish – just don't forget your password!

4 Click **OK**

To de-activate the protection:

1 Open the **Tools** menu and choose **Protection**

2 Select **UnProtect Sheet** (or whatever option is appropriate)

3 If you used a password, you'll be asked to enter it

4 Click **OK**

5.12 Summary

This chapter has concentrated on features that are used when working with formulas and functions. We have discussed:

- AutoSum.
- The Formula Palette.
- The Statistical functions MIN, MAX, AVERAGE and COUNT.
- Viewing the formulas and functions in your worksheet.
- Relative and absolute cell addresses.
- Circular references.
- Named ranges.
- The IF function.
- Adding comments to a cell.
- Cell protection.

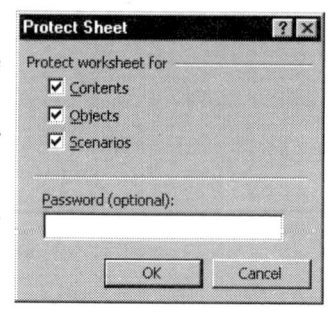

6

CHARTING AND DRAWING

6.1 Aims of this chapter

Pictures often talk louder than words (and numbers). This chapter discusses the charting capabilities in Excel. You'll find Excel has excellent charting facilities – they're easy to use and look great. We'll also take a look at the Drawing toolbar, and see how it can be used to enhance your charts (and data). Have fun!

6.2 Preparing your data

Excel can create charts – bar graphs, line graphs, pie charts, scatter diagrams, etc. – from the data in your worksheet.

You can create your chart on the same worksheet as the data on which the chart is built, or on a separate chart sheet.

- Data that you want to chart should *ideally* be in cells that are adjacent to each other.
- If the data you want to chart has blank rows or columns within it, remove these before you try to chart the data.

To chart data that is not in adjacent cells:

1 Select the first group of cells you want to chart

2 Hold the **[Ctrl]** key down while you click and drag over the other groups you want to include in your chart

- When the non-adjacent cells are selected, the selected areas *must* form a rectangle.

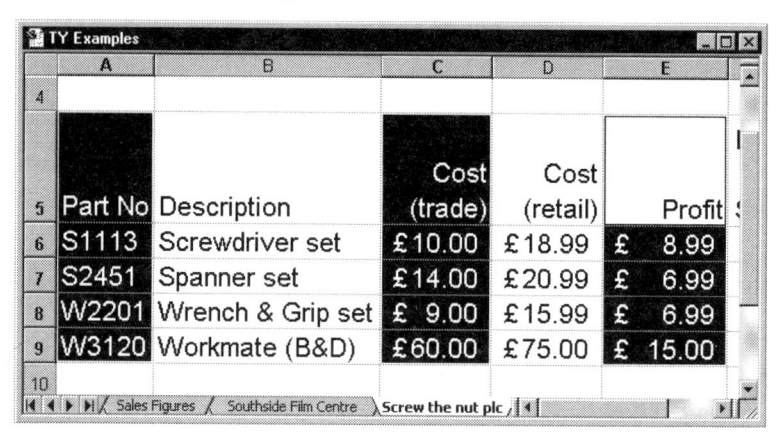

Part No	Description	Cost (trade)	Cost (retail)	Profit
S1113	Screwdriver set	£10.00	£18.99	£ 8.99
S2451	Spanner set	£14.00	£20.99	£ 6.99
W2201	Wrench & Grip set	£ 9.00	£15.99	£ 6.99
W3120	Workmate (B&D)	£60.00	£75.00	£ 15.00

6.3 Chart Wizard

The Chart Wizard is used to step you through the process of setting up your chart.

To chart the data in your worksheet:

1 Select the data you want to chart – including the column headings and row labels

2 Click the **Chart Wizard** tool on the Standard toolbar

3 At step 1 of the Chart Wizard, select the **Chart type**

4 Click the **Press and hold to view sample** button to see what your data would look like in your chosen chart type

5 Once you've decided on a type, click **Next**

CHARTING AND DRAWING

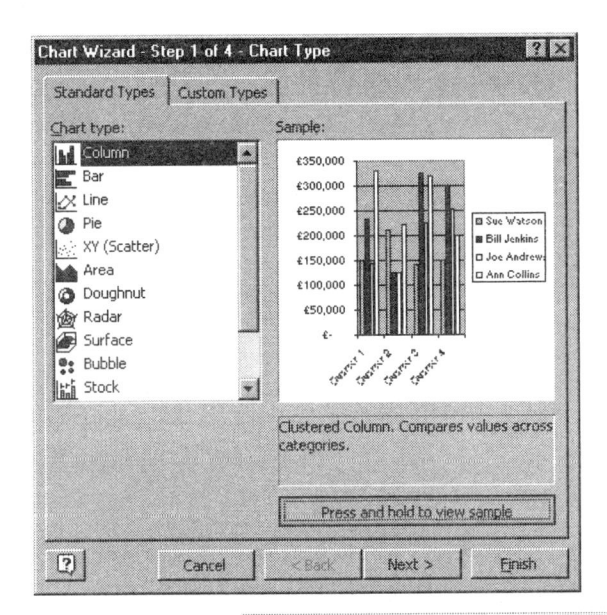

There are many Chart types available, and all types have variations

The preview will show you the effect of your choices

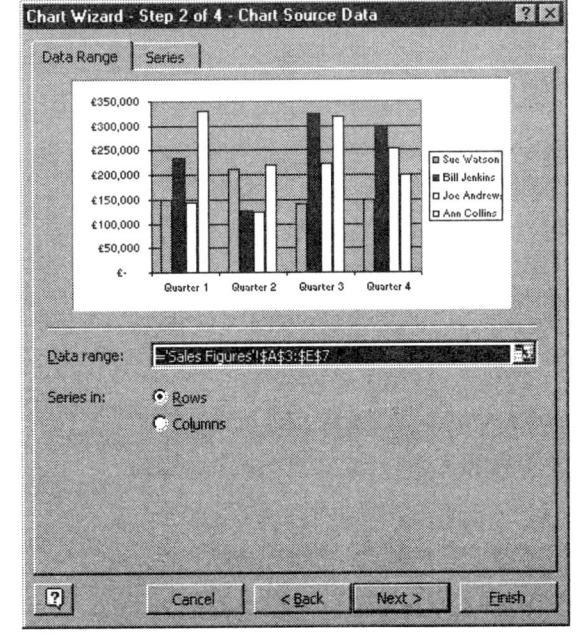

– 101 –

> **USING WIZARDS**
>
> Click [Next >] to move on to the next step in the Wizard, [< Back] to move back to the previous step, [Cancel] if you've changed your mind and want to abandon the WIzard, and [Finish] when you're done.

6 At step 2, on the **Data Range** tab, check the data range selected, decide whether you want to display the data series in rows or columns (try both and decide which you prefer)

- Once a chart has been created, changes made to the data on which the chart is based, will automatically be reflected in the chart. This happens regardless of whether the chart is an object in your worksheet, or on a separate Chart sheet.

7 At step 3, explore the various tabs in the **Chart Options** dialog box and select the options you require. Click **Next** when you want to move on.

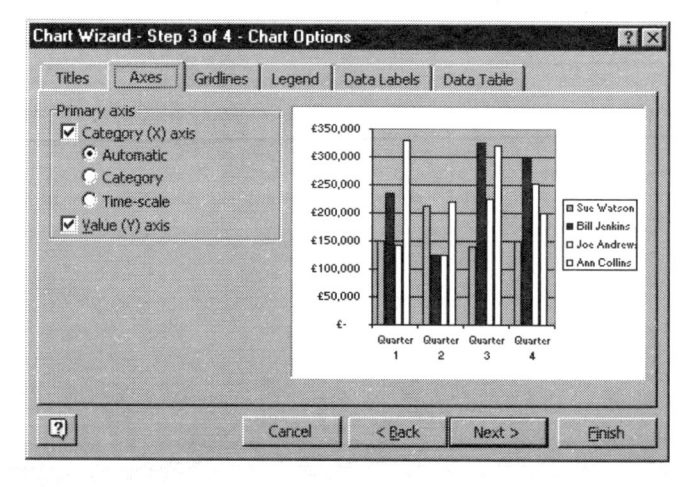

8 Finally, decide where the chart should be located – in your worksheet, or on a separate chart sheet – and click **Finish**

CHARTING AND DRAWING

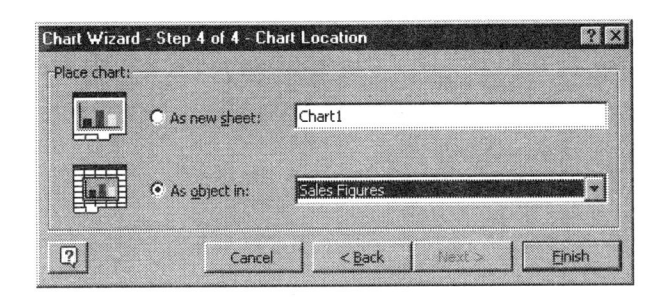

6.4 A chart in your worksheet

If you opt to insert your chart as an object in a worksheet, the Chart toolbar will be displayed when you return to the worksheet.

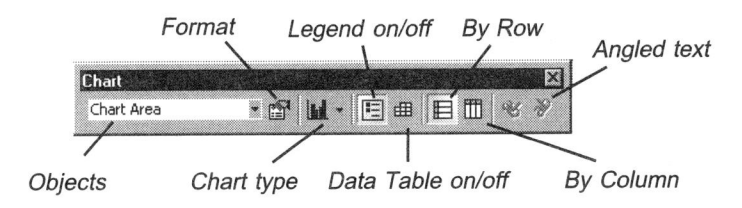

Format   Legend on/off   By Row

Angled text

Objects   Chart type   Data Table on/off   By Column

The chart will be selected – indicated by handles in each corner and along each side. If you click on the worksheet area, the chart becomes de-selected, and the Chart toolbar disappears.

Move, resize and delete chart

If you want to move, resize or delete a chart you must first selected the *Chart Area* – either point to the chart area within the chart and click (a prompt will tell you what the mouse is pointing at) or choose *Chart Area* from the chart object list on the Chart toolbar.

To move the chart:

1 Select the chart

– 103 –

2 Point to the Chart Area using the mouse – a prompt appear to tell you what area of the chart you are pointing at

3 Drag the chart to its new position

To resize the chart:

1 Select the chart

2 Point to one of the handles along the edge of the chart area

3 Drag the handle to increase or decrease the size of the object

To delete the chart:

1 Select the chart

2 Press the **[Delete]** key on your keyboard

Chart objects

Each area of your chart is an object – you have a chart area object, plot area object, category axis object, value axis object, legend object, etc.

To select a chart object:

- Choose the object from the **Chart Objects** list | Legend |

Or

- Click on the object you want to select.

Formatting chart objects

You can change the formatting of each object in your chart to get the effect you want.

To format an object in your chart:

1 Choose the object from the **Chart Objects** list

2 Click the Format tool on the Chart toolbar

Or

1 Double click the chart object you want to format

When the Format dialog box appears, explore it to see the various formatting options you have. Experiment with the options until you find the right formatting for your chart.

- If you want to format the font of an object, you can use the tools on the Formatting toolbar – font, size, bold, italic, etc.

To change the chart type

If your chart doesn't look the way you expected, and you think a different chart type would be better, you can change the chart type at any time.

To change the chart type:

1 Click the drop-down arrow to the right of the **Chart Type** tool on the Chart toolbar

2 Select the type of chart required

Other options

If you explore the menus when your chart is selected, you will find that some of the worksheet menu options have disappeared, and options specific to charting have appeared. The Format menu and Chart menu contain most of the options specific to charting.

In the Chart menu choose:

- **Chart Type...** to return to the dialog box displayed at Step 1 of the Wizard. This dialog box gives you access to all the chart types and sub-types.

- **Source Data...** to return to the dialog box displayed at Step 2 of the Wizard. If you need to edit the data range, this is the best place to do it.

- **Chart Options...** to return to the options displayed at Step 3 of the Wizard. You can add titles, change the position of the legend, edit the gridlines, etc. through this dialog box.

- **Location...** to return to the dialog box displayed at Step 4 of the Wizard. You can change the location of the selected chart from here – useful if you want to move it to another sheet, or decide to put it on a separate chart sheet.

6.5 A chart on a separate sheet

If you opt to locate your chart in a new sheet, your chart will be displayed on a sheet called *Chart1* (unless you've already got a *Chart1* sheet, in which case it will be in the *Chart2* sheet or *Chart3* sheet). The Chart sheet is inserted to the left of the worksheet from which it gets its data.

The Chart toolbar is displayed when the Chart sheet is selected.

You can use the Chart toolbar, or the Format or Chart menu to modify the chart as required.

You can rename the *Chart1* sheet to something more meaningful, move the sheet to another location in your workbook, or delete the chart sheet if you decide you don't need it any more (see Chapter 4 for renaming, moving and deleting sheets).

6.6 Charts without the Wizard

Charts can be created very quickly, missing out the steps you work through with the Chart Wizard. The charts created use the default chart layout – normally a column chart.

To create an embedded chart:
1 Select the cells you want to chart
2 Click the **Default Chart** tool

- If the **Default Chart** tool it not displayed, add it to a toolbar (see Chapter 10).

To create a chart on a separate sheet:
1 Select the cells you want to chart
2 Press **[F11]**

The charts you create can be formatted and printed in the same way as those created using the Chart Wizard.

CHARTING AND DRAWING

6.7 Printing your chart

You can print a chart with or without the data on which it is based.

To print a chart that is an object within your worksheet you have several options. I suggest you do a Print Preview before you actually print, just to check it looks okay.

To print out *all* of the data on the worksheet *and* the chart:
- Print the worksheet as normal (with the chart de-selected)

To get a print out of the chart only:
- Select the chart, then print

To get the chart, plus the data on which it is based, but no other data from the worksheet:
- Display the data table, and print out with the chart selected

To print a chart that is on a separate chart sheet:
1 Select the chart sheet
2 Print as usual

- If you also want to print out the data on which the chart is based, display the data table before you print.

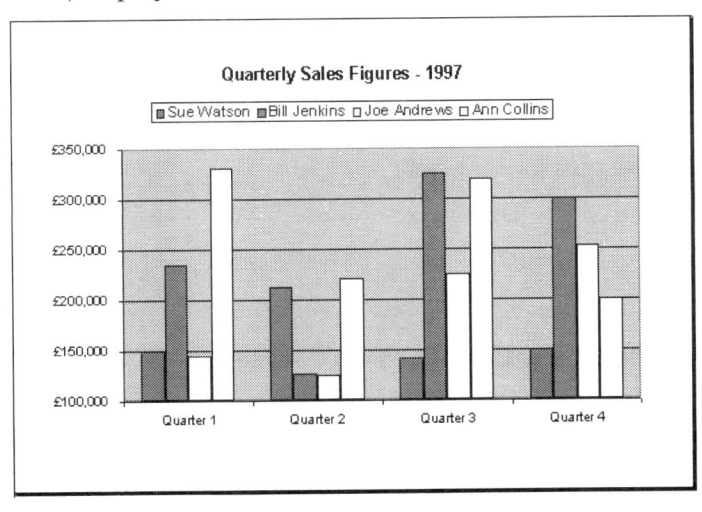

6.8 Default chart

The default chart is a column chart. If you don't use column charts very often, you can change the default chart type.

To change the default chart type:
1 Open the **Chart** menu and choose **Chart Type...**
2 Select the chart type and subtype you want as your default
3 Click the **Set as default chart** button
4 Click **Yes** to change the default, **No** to cancel

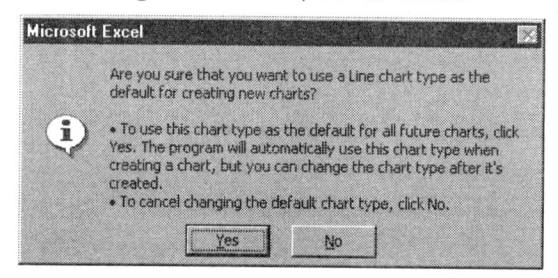

6.9 Drawing tools

You can use the Drawing toolbar to add different effects to your charts (and data). If you want to draw an arrow pointing to an object within your chart, and attach a message to the arrow, you must use the drawing tools.

To display the Drawing toolbar:

- Click the **Drawing** tool on the Standard toolbar.

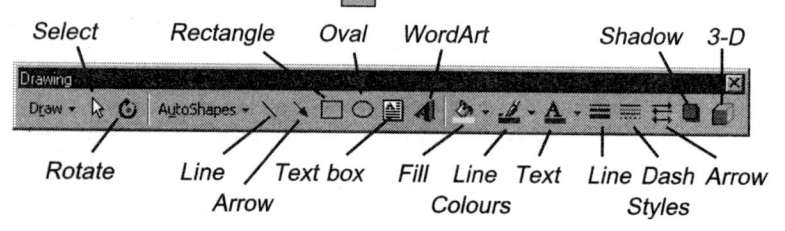

Select Rectangle Oval WordArt Shadow 3-D

Rotate Line Text box Fill Line Text Line Dash Arrow
Arrow Colours Styles

Line, Arrow, Rectangle and Oval

You can use these tools to draw basic lines and shapes.

To use these tools:

1 Click the tool

2 Click and drag to draw

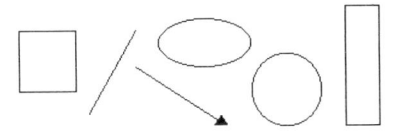

To get a perfect square or circle, select the **Rectangle** or **Oval** tool, and then hold the **[Shift]** key down as you click and drag.

To resize or move your drawing objects:

1 Select the object – click on it

- Click and drag a 'handle' to resize the object
- Click and drag within the object to move it

2 De-select the object

To delete a drawing object:

1 Select the object and press the **[Delete]** key

To add a shadow or 3-D effect to your object:

1 Select the object

2 Click the **Shadow** tool or **3-D** tool

3 Choose the effect you want

4 De-select the object

To change a line or arrow style of an object:

1 Select the object you want to change

2 Click the **Line style**, **Dash style** or **Arrow style** tool

3 Choose the effect you want

4 De-select the object

To change the fill colour or line colour of an object:

1 Select the object

2 Click the drop-down arrow on the **Fill** or **Line color** tool

3 Choose a colour

4 De-select the object

Text Boxes

Text Boxes let you add text anywhere in your worksheet.

To insert a Text Box:

1 Click the **Text Box** tool

2 Click and drag within your worksheet to create a Text Box

3 Type in the text you want to appear in the Text Box

4 De-select the object

AutoShapes

If you want to draw stars, banners, block arrows, flow chart symbols, etc. you may find the shape you need in the AutoShapes. These are just as easy to use as the basic shapes above.

1 Click the **AutoShapes** tool

2 Choose a category

3 Select a shape

4 Click and drag to draw the shape

- The **Callouts** are a variation on Text Boxes – see above.

Callout

CHARTING AND DRAWING

6.10 Some more options

The Draw tool on the Drawing toolbar gives access to yet more options. Some of them are introduced here.

Grouping

If you are drawing a picture using different drawing objects, you will find your final picture easier to resize and move if you *Group* the objects together.

Before you can group several objects, you must select them.

To select more than one object at a time:

1. Select the first object required – click on it
2. Hold the **[Shift]** key down while you click on each of the other objects

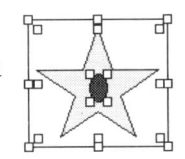

Or

1. Click the **Select Objects** tool on the Drawing toolbar
2. Click and drag over the objects you want to select

To group objects:

1. Select the objects you want to group
2. Click the drop-down arrow to the right of **Draw** on the Drawing toolbar
3. Choose **Group**

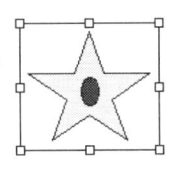

The objects are grouped together into one object and can then be resized, moved or deleted as one. If you need to work on a component, you can ungroup the object again.

To ungroup an object: *rewrite*

1. Select the object you want to ungroup
2. Click the drop-down arrow to the right of **Draw**
3. Choose **Ungroup**

To regroup objects than have been ungrouped:

1 Click the drop-down arrow to the right of **Draw**

2 Choose **Regroup**

- Objects that have been ungrouped are automatically regrouped.

Bring Forward, Send Backward

When you draw your objects on top of each other, the first one you draw is on the lowest layer, the second one is on a layer above the first one, the third one on the next layer and so on.

If you end up with your objects on the wrong layer relative to each other, you can move them backwards and forwards through the layers as necessary.

To move an object from one layer to another:

1 Select the object

2 Choose **Order** from the **Draw** drop-down list

3 Move the object backwards or forwards as required

- **Bring to Front** and **Send to Back** move the object to the top or bottom layer respectively.

- **Bring Forward** and **Send Backward** move the object one layer at a time.

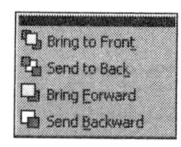

Rotate & Flip

Objects can also be rotated by any amount, or flipped 180 degrees horizontally or vertically.

To rotate an object:

1 Select the object

2 Click the **Free Rotate** tool on the Drawing toolbar

3 Click and drag the rotate handles (small green circles) until the object is in the position required

4 Select another tool or click **Free Rotate** again to end

To flip an object:

1 Select the object
2 Choose **Rotate** or **Flip** from the **Draw** drop-down list
3 Select a rotate or flip option

You can use the drawing tools to create different effects on your worksheet data and charts. If you create charts, try using an Arrow and a Text box to add emphasis to it!

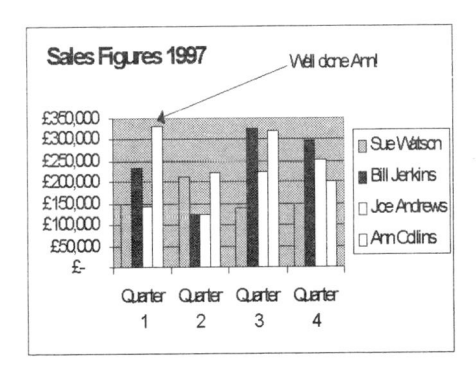

6.11 Summary

In this chapter we have discussed some of the options available when creating and editing charts in Excel. We have considered:

- Preparing data for charting.
- The Chart Wizard.
- Embedded charts.
- Charts on separate sheets.
- Producing charts without using the Chart Wizard.
- Printing charts.
- Changing the default chart.
- The Drawing toolbar.

7
AUTOFORMAT, STYLES AND TEMPLATES

7.1 Aims of this chapter

In this chapter we will discuss some of the ways you can automate the formatting and page layout of your worksheet. We considered several formatting and page layout options in Chapter 3. In this chapter we will discuss how AutoFormat, Styles and Templates can make you more efficient when formatting.

7.2 AutoFormat

Instead of formatting your worksheet manually (as discussed in Chapter 3), you could try the AutoFormats. The AutoFormats are layouts that are already set up in Excel, and they can be applied to any area of your worksheet.

If you don't select an area of your worksheet before applying an AutoFormat, Excel will apply it to everything surrounding the current cell, until it reaches an empty row and/or column.

If you want to apply the AutoFormat to an area that includes empty rows and/or columns, you must select the whole area first.

To apply an AutoFormat:

1 Select the area (if necessary)

2 Open the **Format** menu and choose **AutoFormat...**

3 Scroll through the list and choose a format

4 Click the **Options** button and select or de-select any options you don't want to apply

5 Click **OK**

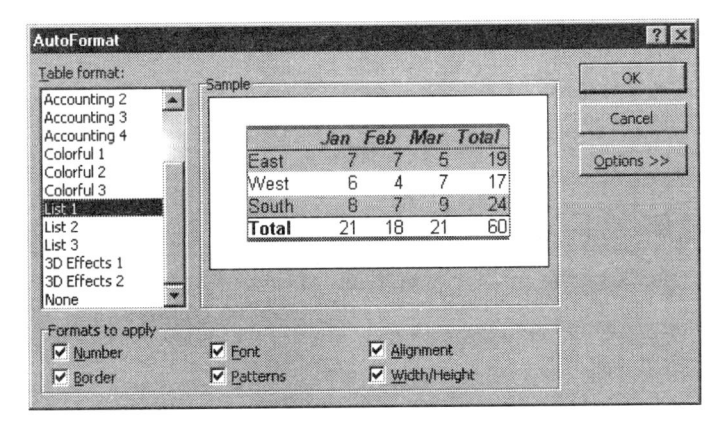

7.3 Introducing styles

A style is a set of formatting options that you save as a group. When you want to apply the formats held in a style, you apply the style rather than each formatting option individually.

If you don't apply a style to the text or data you enter into your worksheet, it is formatted using the Normal style.

If you format your data using the Currency, Comma or Percent style tools on the Formatting toolbar you are applying a style that has already been set up in Excel.

Other styles that have already been set up in Excel are Currency styles (with 0 decimal places) and Comma styles (with 0 decimal places).

Using styles has two main benefits:

- **Consistency** – when you apply a style all the formatting options contained within it are applied in one go (you won't accidentally use the wrong font size or colour).

- **Speed** – it's usually quicker to apply a style than it is to apply formatting options using the Format Cells dialog box.

7.4 Working with styles

You can apply existing styles to your cells, edit existing styles, create styles of your own and delete styles you no longer use.

To apply an existing style:

1 Select the range of cells you want to format
2 Choose **Style...** from the **Format** menu
3 Select the style you want to use from the **Style name** list
4 Click **OK**

The Style can cover all aspects of formatting

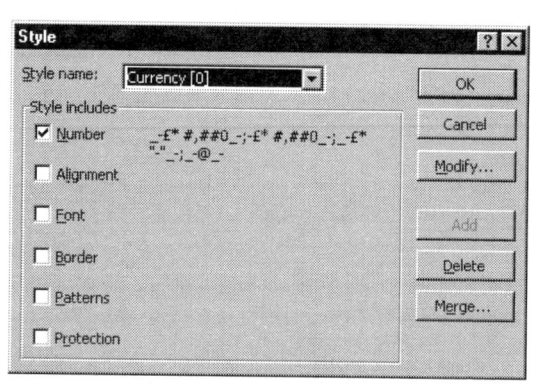

- You can click the style tools on the Formatting toolbar to apply **Currency**, **Comma**, and **Percent** styles.

To edit an existing style:

1 Choose **Style...** from the **Format** menu

2. Select the style you want to edit from the **Style name** list
3. Click the **Modify** button
4. Make the changes required in the **Format Cells** dialog box
5. Click **OK** to return to the **Style** dialog box
6. Click **OK** to return to your worksheet

To create a new style:

1. Select a cell (or cells) that has the combination of formats you want to record into a style
2. Choose **Style...** from the **Format** menu
3. Enter a new name for the style in the **Style name** list box
4. Click **Add** to add the style to the list without applying the style to the selected cell, then click **Close**

Or

- Click **OK** to add the style to the list and apply it to the cells.

To delete a style:

1. Choose **Style...** from the **Format** menu
2. Select the style you want to delete from the **Style name** list
3. Click the **Delete** button

- You cannot delete the *Normal* style.

- If you delete the *Currency*, *Comma* or *Percent* style, you will not be able to use their tools on the Formatting toolbar.

If you have styles already set up in one workbook, and want to use them in another workbook, you can copy the styles over.

To copy styles from one workbook to another:

1. Open the workbook that contains the styles you want to copy
2. Open the workbook that you want to copy the styles into
3. Choose **Style...** from the **Format** menu
4. Click the **Merge** button

5 Double click the workbook with the styles you want to copy

- If the destination workbook already contains styles of the same name as those being copied in, you will be asked to confirm whether or not you want the styles copied.

6 Click **OK**

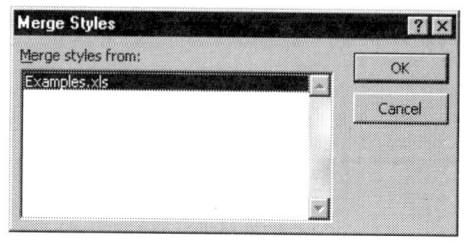

- Styles can be applied and edited from the Style Box. If you intend to use styles, I suggest you add the Style Box to one of your toolbars, (see Section 10.4).

7.5 Workbook templates

A template is the pattern on which your workbook or worksheet is based. Up until now, your workbooks have been based on the default template. The default workbook template is the one used to create a new workbook when you start Excel, or when you click the New tool on the Standard toolbar, or choose Workbook from the General tab in the New dialog box.

If you create different workbooks that follow the same basic layout, you could create a *custom* template for these workbooks. The custom template would contain the elements of your workbooks that are standard, e.g. standard text, column headings and row labels, formulas, functions, headers/footers, styles, etc.

To create a custom workbook template:

1 Create a new workbook
2 Insert or delete sheets as necessary to get the number of sheets you require in this template

AUTOFORMAT, STYLES AND TEMPLATES

3   Add any standard text, formatting, formulas, functions, headers/footers, styles, etc. to the workbook

4   If you want a preview of your workbook to be displayed in the **New** dialog box, choose **Properties** from the **File** menu. On the **Summary** tab in the **Properties** dialog box, select the **Save preview picture** checkbox and click **OK**.

5   Click the **Save** tool on the **Standard** toolbar

6   In the **Save as File type** field, choose **Template**

7   Select the *Templates* folder in the *MSOffice* folder (or *Microsoft Excel* folder if you don't have Office) in the **Save in** field

8   Type in a name for the template in the **File name** field

9   Click **Save**

10 Close your template when you've finished

To create a new workbook using your custom template:

1   Choose **New** from the **File** menu

2   Select your template from the **General** tab in the **New** dialog box

3   Click **OK**

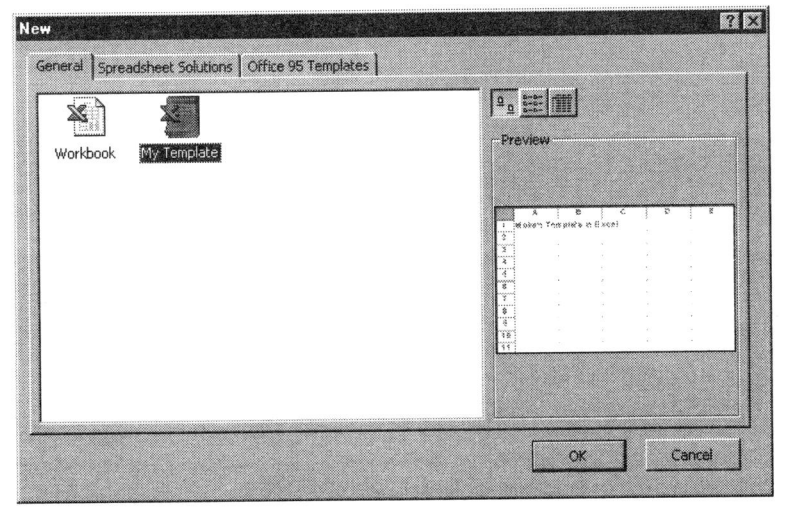

If you want to make a custom workbook template the default workbook template, you can do so.

To create the default workbook template:

1 Follow steps 1–6 in the **create a custom workbook template** instructions above

2 Select the *XLStart* folder in the *Office* folder in the *MSOffice* folder, e.g. *C:MSOffice\Office\XLStart* (or in the *Microsoft Excel* folder) or the alternate startup folder (see below)

3 In the **File name** field, type *Book* (this is the template name Excel will look for when it starts up)

4 Click **Save**

5 Close your template when you've finished

ALTERNATE STARTUP FOLDER

The contents of the XLStart folder are opened automatically when you go into Excel (that's why you put your default template book in it if you want to change the default workbook). However, you can specify an alternative folder as your startup folder if you wish - this folder is known as the Alternate Startup Folder. You can specify your Alternate Startup Folder location on the General tab in the Options dialog box.

7.6 Worksheet templates

You can create templates for the sheets you add to workbooks.

To create a custom worksheet template:

1 Create a new workbook consisting of ONE sheet only

2 Add any standard text, formatting, formulas, functions, headers/footers, styles, etc. to the worksheet

AUTOFORMAT, STYLES AND TEMPLATES

3 If you want a preview of your worksheet to be displayed in the **Insert** dialog box, choose **Properties** from the **File** menu. On the **Summary** tab in the **Properties** dialog box, select the **Save preview picture** checkbox and click **OK**.

4 Click the **Save** tool on the **Standard** toolbar

5 In the **Save as File type** field, choose *Template*

6 Select the *Templates* folder in the *MSOffice* folder or *Microsoft Excel* folder in the **Save in** field

7 Type in a name for the template in the **File name** field

8 Click **Save**

9 Close the worksheet template

To insert a custom worksheet template:

1 Right click on a sheet tab and select **Insert...** from the pop-up menu

2 Select your worksheet template from the **General** tab in the **Insert** dialog box

3 Click **OK**

The new sheet will be inserted to the left of the selected one.

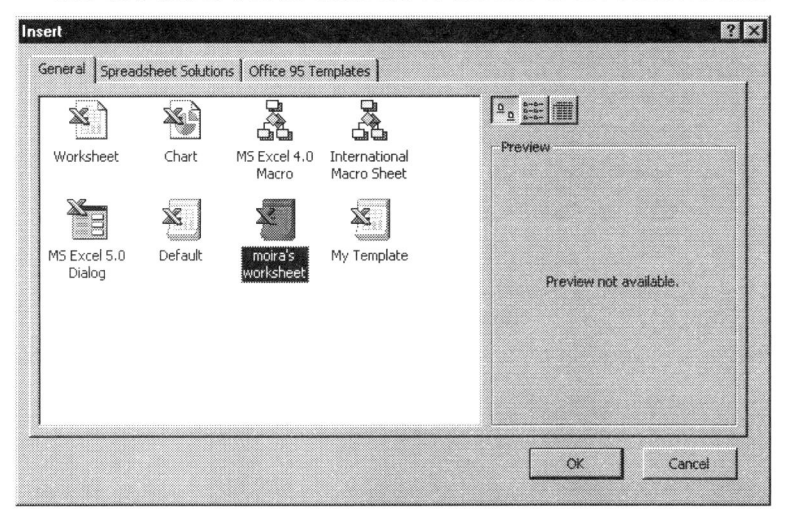

7.7 Summary

This chapter has discussed some of the ways you can automate the way you work in Excel. We have considered:

- AutoFormat.
- Using standard Excel styles.
- Editing styles.
- Creating your own styles.
- Designing a custom workbook template.
- Creating a new workbook using your custom template.
- Changing the default workbook template.
- Creating a custom worksheet template.
- Inserting the custom worksheet template into your workbook.

8

DATABASE FEATURES

8.1 Aims of this chapter

This chapter introduces the database capabilities of Excel. Sort, AutoFilter, Advanced Filter and Data validation will all be discussed.

8.2 Database terminology

In Excel, a list of data in your worksheet can be used as a database. Lists of stock items, customer names and phone numbers, student exam results, etc. can all be manipulated using the database feature in Excel.

Database functions such as sort, find and filter can be performed on your lists. When using your list as a database:

- Each row is considered to be a *record* in your database.
- Each column is a *field*.
- The column headings are your *field names*.

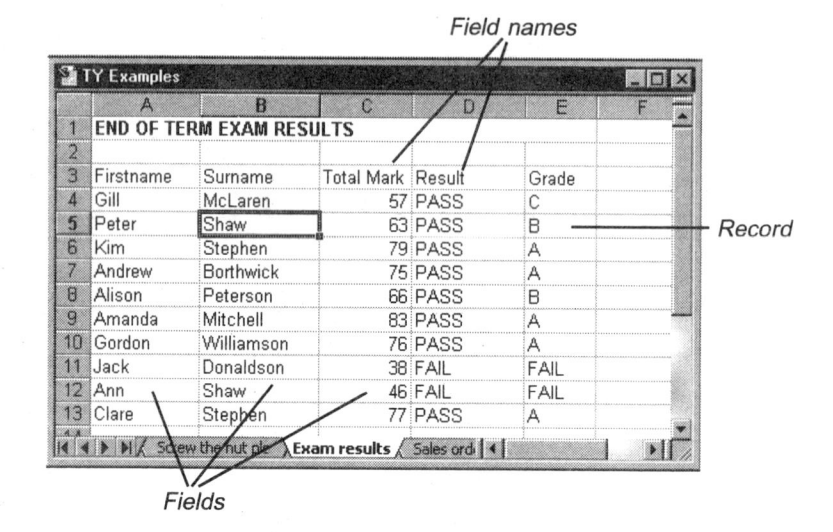

Field names

	A	B	C	D	E	F
1	END OF TERM EXAM RESULTS					
2						
3	Firstname	Surname	Total Mark	Result	Grade	
4	Gill	McLaren	57	PASS	C	
5	Peter	Shaw	63	PASS	B	
6	Kim	Stephen	79	PASS	A	
7	Andrew	Borthwick	75	PASS	A	
8	Alison	Peterson	66	PASS	B	
9	Amanda	Mitchell	83	PASS	A	
10	Gordon	Williamson	76	PASS	A	
11	Jack	Donaldson	38	FAIL	FAIL	
12	Ann	Shaw	46	FAIL	FAIL	
13	Clare	Stephen	77	PASS	A	

Record

Fields

8.3 Sort

The data in your worksheet can be sorted into ascending or descending order. You can perform a simple sort on the data, where you sort the data using the entries in one column only, or a more complex sort where you can sort on up to 3 columns at a time.

When you sort your data, the rows and columns surrounding the current cell will be included in the sort. When performing a simple sort on a list of data, there should be no blank rows or columns inside the area you want to sort.

Excel assumes that the first row of the data you want to sort is a header row (with column labels in it) and doesn't include it in the sort.

To perform a simple sort:

1 Select any cell in the column you want to base your sort on

2 Click the **Sort Ascending** or **Sort Descending** tool on the Standard toolbar

DATABASE FEATURES

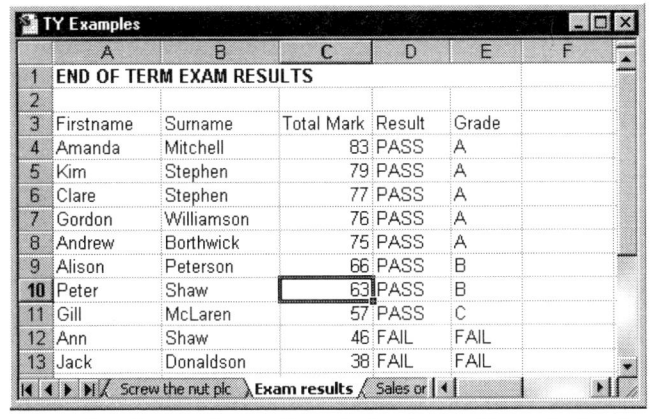

	A	B	C	D	E	F
1	END OF TERM EXAM RESULTS					
2						
3	Firstname	Surname	Total Mark	Result	Grade	
4	Amanda	Mitchell	83	PASS	A	
5	Kim	Stephen	79	PASS	A	
6	Clare	Stephen	77	PASS	A	
7	Gordon	Williamson	76	PASS	A	
8	Andrew	Borthwick	75	PASS	A	
9	Alison	Peterson	66	PASS	B	
10	Peter	Shaw	63	PASS	B	
11	Gill	McLaren	57	PASS	C	
12	Ann	Shaw	46	FAIL	FAIL	
13	Jack	Donaldson	38	FAIL	FAIL	

The example above shows the student result worksheet sorted into descending order on the *Total Mark* column.

To perform a multi-level sort:

1 Select any cell within the group of cells you want sorted

2 Open the **Data** menu and choose **Sort...**

3 Select the main sort field from the **Sort by** list

4 Choose the order – **Ascending** or **Descending**

5 Select the second level sort field from the first **Then by** list, and set its sort order

6 If necessary, set the third level sort options

7 Click **OK**

– 125 –

- Note that by default, Excel assumes your list has a *Header row*. The Header row is the row that normally contains the column labels or field names. If your list doesn't have a header row, i.e. you want the first row included in the sort, select the **No header row** option.

	A	B	C	D	E
1	END OF TERM EXAM RESULTS				
2					
3	Firstname	Surname	Total Mark	Result	Grade
4	Andrew	Borthwick	75	PASS	A
5	Jack	Donaldson	38	FAIL	FAIL
6	Gill	McLaren	57	PASS	C
7	Amanda	Mitchell	83	PASS	A
8	Alison	Peterson	66	PASS	B
9	Ann	Shaw	46	FAIL	FAIL
10	Peter	Shaw	63	PASS	B
11	Clare	Stephen	77	PASS	A
12	Kim	Stephen	79	PASS	A
13	Gordon	Williamson	76	PASS	A

- The list in the example above has been sorted into *Surname* order (ascending) then *Firstname* order (ascending).

You can also use the Sort feature to rearrange the columns in your worksheet. To do this, the columns must be numbered in the order you want them to be in.

To rearrange the columns:

1 In the row immediately above (or below) your list, type in numbers to indicate the order you want the columns to be in.

2 Select any cell in the list you want to sort.

3 Open the **Data** menu and choose **Sort...**

4 Click **Options...**

5 Select **Sort left to right** in the **Orientation** options and click **OK**

6 In the **Sort by** field, indicate the row number that has the entries you want to sort (row 3 in this example)

DATABASE FEATURES

	A	B	C	D	E	F
1	END OF TERM EXAM RESULTS					
2						
3	2	1	3	4	5	
4	Firstname	Surname	Total Mark	Result	Grade	
5	Andrew	Borthwick	75	PASS	A	
6	Jack	Donaldson	38	FAIL	FAIL	
7	Gill	McLaren	57	PASS	C	
8	Amanda	Mitchell	83	PASS	A	
9	Alison	Peterson	66	PASS	B	
10	Ann	Shaw	46	FAIL	FAIL	
11	Peter	Shaw	63	PASS	B	
12	Clare	Stephen	77	PASS	A	
13	Kim	Stephen	79	PASS	A	
14	Gordon	Williamson	76	PASS	A	

7 Click **OK**

- Once your data has been sorted, you can delete the row that contains the numbers.

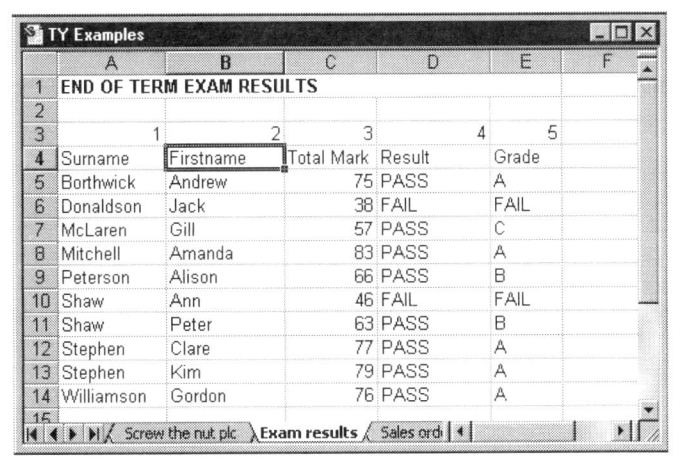

	A	B	C	D	E	F
1	END OF TERM EXAM RESULTS					
2						
3	1	2	3	4	5	
4	Surname	Firstname	Total Mark	Result	Grade	
5	Borthwick	Andrew	75	PASS	A	
6	Donaldson	Jack	38	FAIL	FAIL	
7	McLaren	Gill	57	PASS	C	
8	Mitchell	Amanda	83	PASS	A	
9	Peterson	Alison	66	PASS	B	
10	Shaw	Ann	46	FAIL	FAIL	
11	Shaw	Peter	63	PASS	B	
12	Stephen	Clare	77	PASS	A	
13	Stephen	Kim	79	PASS	A	
14	Williamson	Gordon	76	PASS	A	

Circular references

If you try to sort columns that have formulas in them, you may run into problems with circular references where you end up with a formula in a cell that points to the cell itself. If this occurs, edit the formula as necessary to get rid of the circular reference.

If you create a circular reference, the prompt below will appear. Respond to the prompt as appropriate to your circumstances. (See 5.7 for more information.)

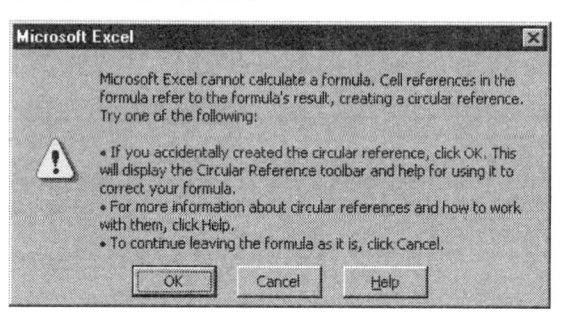

8.4 AutoFilter

You may want to display only the records from your list that meet specific criteria. You can use the AutoFilter to quickly filter out the records you don't want to see, and display only those that meet the criteria you specify.

To switch the AutoFilter on:

1 Select a cell within the list you want to work with

2 Open the **Data** menu, choose **Filter**, than **AutoFilter**

- Each field name (column heading) becomes a combo box (drop-down list), with a drop-down arrow to the right of it.

To view records that contain a specific value:

1 Click the drop-down arrow to the right of the field name you want to select on

2 Select the value you want to view the records for

3 If you want to filter the result further, based on a value in another column, repeat steps 1 and 2 in the other column

In this example, the students who have an A in the *Grade* column have been selected.

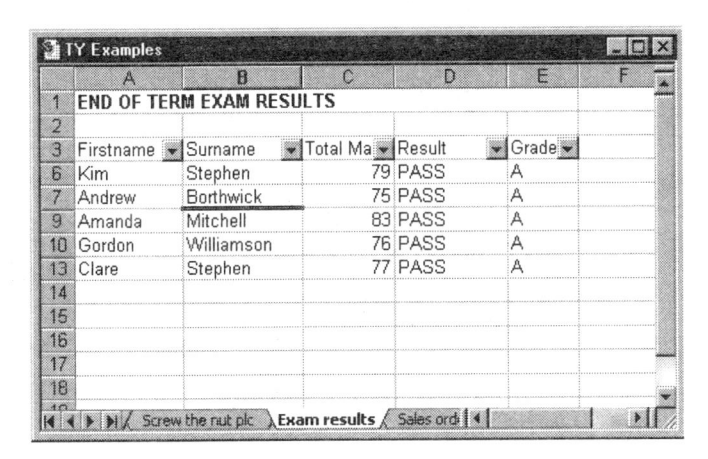

	A	B	C	D	E	F
1	END OF TERM EXAM RESULTS					
2						
3	Firstname	Surname	Total Ma	Result	Grade	
6	Kim	Stephen	79	PASS	A	
7	Andrew	Borthwick	75	PASS	A	
9	Amanda	Mitchell	83	PASS	A	
10	Gordon	Williamson	76	PASS	A	
13	Clare	Stephen	77	PASS	A	

The column or columns that you have specified your criteria in have a blue arrow to the right of the field name so you can identify which columns have conditions set in them.

- By default, AutoFilter will list records that are *equal* to the criteria you have selected. If you want a different operator, e.g. *does not equal*, you must use the **Custom AutoFilter** dialog box. To open the dialog box, choose (**Custom...**) from the drop-down list.

To display all the records again:

1 Click the drop-down arrow on the column(s) that have criteria set

2 Choose (**All**) from the list of options

Or

1 Open the **Data** menu and select **Filter**

2 Choose **Show All**

You can use AutoFilter to filter a list by up to two values in the same column. To do so you must set up a *Custom filter*.

To filter a list by two values in the same column:

1 Click the drop-down arrow to the right of the field name you want to select on

2 Select (**Custom...**)

3 At the **Custom AutoFilter** dialog box, set up the criteria required – in this case we are looking for students who have either a *C* grade or a *Fail*

4 Click **OK**

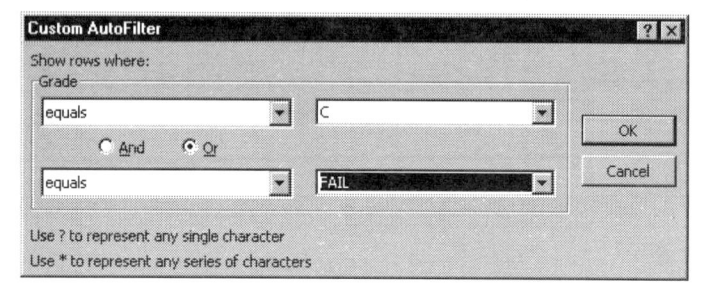

- The list of records matching your criteria will be displayed.

If you want to list all students who have more than a certain score in the *Total Mark* column, you must use the Custom AutoFilter (e. g. *Total Mark is greater than 55*). If you want all students whose surname falls within the range M-S (*Surname is greater than L, and is less than T*), you must use the Custom AutoFilter.

8.5 Advanced Filter

If you want to use several criteria to filter your data, or if you want to keep a set of criteria for future use, you must use the Advanced Filter.

The Advanced Filter requires you to specify the criteria you wish to apply on a separate area of the worksheet. The criteria in this range – which is called the *criteria range* – are then applied your list of data.

You must set up your criteria range first, then apply it to your list of data.

DATABASE FEATURES

To set up the criteria range:

1 Copy the column headings or field names to a blank area in your worksheet

2 Specify the criteria required in the rows under the copied column headings

- If you enter several conditions in one row, Excel will only return a record where the first condition AND the second condition AND the third condition, etc. are met – in other words *all* the conditions must be met in a single record before a record is returned.

- If you enter the conditions in different rows, Excel will return a record that meets one condition *or* the other.

The picture below gives examples of valid criteria.

- The first one will list only those who have the surname *Stephen* OR *Shaw*.

- The second one will list all whose *Surname* falls between M and the end of the alphabet, AND have 70 or more in the *Total Mark* column.

- The third one lists all whose *Surname* starts with an A-G.

- The fourth one lists all the *Shaws* who have not failed.

F	G	H	I	J	K	L
2						
3	Firstname	Surname	Total Mark	Result	Grade	
4		Stephen				
5		Shaw				
6						
7	Firstname	Surname	Total Mark	Result	Grade	
8		>=M	>=70			
9						
10	Firstname	Surname	Surname	Total Mark	Result	Grade
11		>=A	<=G			
12						
13	Firstname	Surname	Total Mark	Result	Grade	
14		Shaw			<>FAIL	
15						

To apply the conditions set in the criteria range:

1 Select any cell in the list of data from which you want to extract records

2 Open the **Data** menu and choose **Filter**, then **Advanced Filter**

3 Do you want to **Filter the list in place**, or **Copy to another location**, in a separate area of the worksheet, those records that match the criteria – select the option required

4 Specify the **List range** – the cells you want to extract records from. Excel should suggest the range you have selected a cell within; correct the range if necessary.

5 Indicate the **Criteria range** – the cells that hold the criteria you want applied. The range should include the field names as well as the criteria. Do not include any blank rows in the criteria area.

6 If you want the result to appear in a different location to the original list, indicate the reference of the cell that will be in the top left corner of the area you want to **Copy to**.

7 Click **OK**

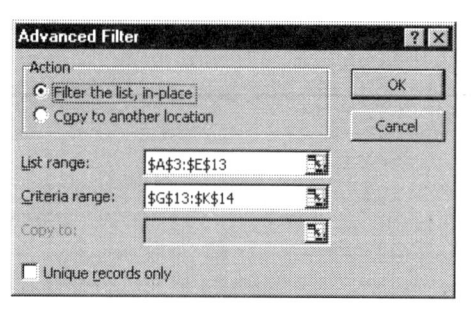

If you opted to filter the list in place, to display all the records again:

- Open the **Data** menu, choose **Filter** then select **Show All**.

DATABASE FEATURES

8.6 Data validation

When entering data into a worksheet, you will want to try to ensure, as far as is practicable, that the data is accurate. To help achieve this, you can set up validation rules for any cell or range where you want to check the validity of the data entered.

By default, each cell in your worksheet will accept any value you enter into it. However, you can limit the range of acceptable entries by setting up validation rules.

Let's say, in our Exam Results example, that we decided to set a validation rule for the data area in the *Total Mark* column so that it would accept values between 0 and 100 only. Anything over 100, or less than 0, would not be accepted and an error message would appear.

To set a validation rule:

1 Select the cell or cells you want the rule to apply to (don't include the column heading or any cells you *don't* want the rule to apply to)

2 Open the **Data** menu and choose **Validation...**

3 On the **Settings** tab, complete the validation criteria fields

4 If you want an **Input message** displayed when the cell is selected, enter it on the **Input Message** tab

5 If you want a specific **Error message** to appear when the validation rule is not met, enter it on the **Error Alert** tab (a default message appears if you don't set up your own)

6 Click **OK** when you're finished

- When you select a cell on your worksheet that has the validation rule applied to it, the input message you set up on the Input Message tab will be displayed.

- If you enter invalid data into a cell that has a validation rule applied to it, the message you set up on the Error Alert tab will appear (or the default error alert message will appear if you didn't specify your own one).

Set the criteria for valid data

Type an input message if wanted

Remove the checks from selected cells

Type an error message if wanted

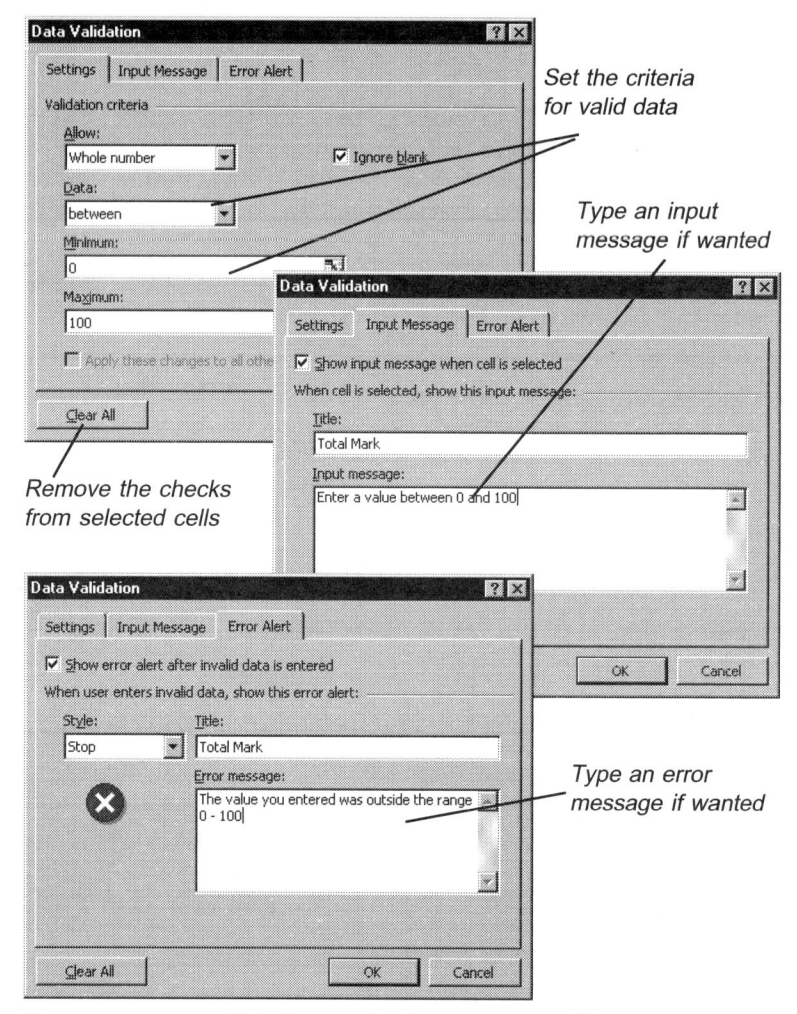

To remove a validation rule from your cells:

1 Select the cell(s) from which you want to remove the rule

2 Open the **Data** menu and choose **Validation...**

3 Click the **Clear All** button

4 Click **OK**

DATABASE FEATURES

8.7 Data form

As an alternative to displaying the data in your worksheet as a list, you may find a form easier to work with. A form displays one record, or row, from your list at a time, rather than as many records as will fit on your screen.

To display your data in a form:

1 Select any cell in the list of data you want to display in a form

2 Open the **Data** menu and choose **Form...**

The first record in the list of data will be displayed.

Fields that you can enter data into or edit are displayed as text boxes – *Firstname*, *Surname* and *Total Mark* in this example.

Calculated fields have their value displayed, but you cannot enter or edit the entry in them directly.

To add a new record:

- Click the **New** button and complete the blank form.

To delete a record:

- Display the record you want to delete and click the **Delete** button. Confirm the deletion at the prompt if you are sure that you want to go ahead and remove the record.

If you edit the contents of a field, then realise you shouldn't have, you can restore the fields to hold the data, as it was when you accessed the record. Restore only works if you have *not* left the record. If you make changes, go to another record, then return to the edited record, you will have to manually update the fields.

To restore a record:

- Click the **Restore** button.

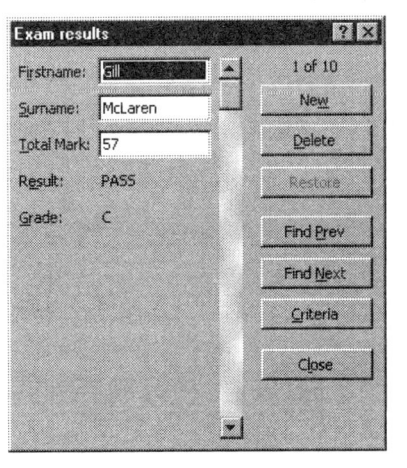

To move from one record to another:

- Click the **Find Prev** or **Find Next** button to move back and forward through the records.

To display records that meet specific criteria:

1 Click the **Criteria** button

2 Complete the fields with the criteria you want to apply

3 Click the **Form** button to leave the **Criteria** dialog box

4 Use **Find Prev** or **Find Next** to view the selected records

To cancel the criteria that have been set:

1 Click the **Criteria** button

2 Delete the criteria

3 Click the **Form** button to leave the **Criteria** dialog box

To return to your worksheet:

- Click the **Close** button.

8.8 Summary

This chapter has discussed how you work with a list of entries in a worksheet using database type features. We have considered:

- Database terminology and how it relates to Excel terminology.
- Sorting into ascending or descending order by a simple sort.
- Multi-level sorts.
- Using Sort to rearrange columns.
- Locating data using the AutoFilter.
- Locating data using the Advanced Filter.
- Validation rules.
- Displaying your list as a simple form.

9

MACROS

9.1 Aims of this chapter

We have already discussed some of the features that can be used to help you automate the way you work in Excel – AutoFormat, Styles, Templates, etc. In this chapter we will consider how macros can help you automate your work. Macros are useful when you want to automate a *routine* that you perform regularly. In this chapter we will discuss some areas in which you may find macros useful. You will learn how to record, play back and edit the macros you create.

9.2 What are macros?

A macro is a set of Excel commands grouped together so that you can execute them as a single command.

If you perform a task often, but cannot find an Excel keyboard shortcut, or tool, that runs through the sequence you want to use, you should record the commands into a macro. You have then created a 'custom' command.

What could you use a macro for?

- Speeding up routine editing and formatting.
- Recording the instructions to create a new document using one of your templates – your budget or monthly sales figures.
- Quickly accessing an option you regularly use in a dialog box.
- Combining a group of commands you often execute in the same sequence.

There are two ways to create macros in Excel:

- **Macro Recorder** – we will be using this option. You can use the Macro Recorder to record any function that you can access through the menus and dialog boxes.
- **Visual Basic Editor** – you can record powerful, flexible macros using the Visual Basic Editor. These macros can include Visual Basic commands as well as Excel commands. We will take a brief excursion into the Visual Basic Editor when we discuss editing macros.

9.3 Recording your macro

Before you start recording your macro, think through what it is that you want to record. If there are any commands that you're not sure about, try them out first to check that they do what you want to record.

Try recording a macro to display the formulas in a worksheet.

To display the formulas, you must:

1 Choose **Options** from the **Tools** menu
2 Select the **Formulas** checkbox on the **View** tab
3 Click **OK**

Once you know what you need to record, re-set the checkbox on the View tab, then record your macro.

To re-set the checkbox:

1 Open the **Tools** menu and choose **Options**
2 De-select the **Formulas** checkbox on the **View** tab
3 Click **OK**

To record the macro:

1 Open the **Tools** menu, choose **Macro** then **Record New Macro...**

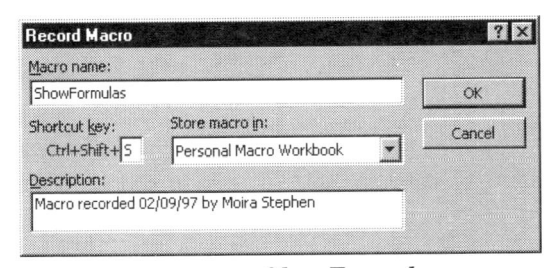

2 Give your macro a name, e.g. *ShowFormulas*.

- Don't use spaces in the macro name. If you want to separate words, use the underline character or a full stop.

3 If you want a keyboard shortcut, click in the **Shortcut** field and enter the shortcut you want to use, e.g. *Ctrl+Shift+S*

4 Select the workbook you want to store the macro in

- If you choose the *Personal Macro Workbook*, your macro will be globally available, in every workbook you create.

5 Click **OK**

- You will be returned to your worksheet, and the **Stop Recording** toolbar will be displayed.

6 Work through the steps you want to record
7 Click the **Stop** tool when you've finished

Create a new macro, this time to switch Formula View off:

1 Open the **Tools** menu, choose **Macro** then **Record New Macro...**
2 Give your macro a name – *HideFormulas* would be okay

3 If you want a keyboard shortcut, click in the **Shortcut** field and enter the shortcut you want to use, e.g. *Ctrl+Shift+H*

4 Select the workbook you want to store the macro in

5 Click **OK**

6 Work through the steps you want to record

7 Click the **Stop** tool when you've finished

9.4 Playing back your macro

You can play back a macro with the keyboard shortcut, if you created one, or through the Tools menu.

To use the keyboard shortcut:

- Press the keyboard shortcut you recorded, e.g. *Ctrl+Shift+S* to show the formulas and *Ctrl+Shift+H* to hide them again.

To use the Tools menu:

1 Open the **Tools** menu and choose **Macro**

2 Select **Macros...**

3 At the **Macro** dialog box, select the macro and click **Run**

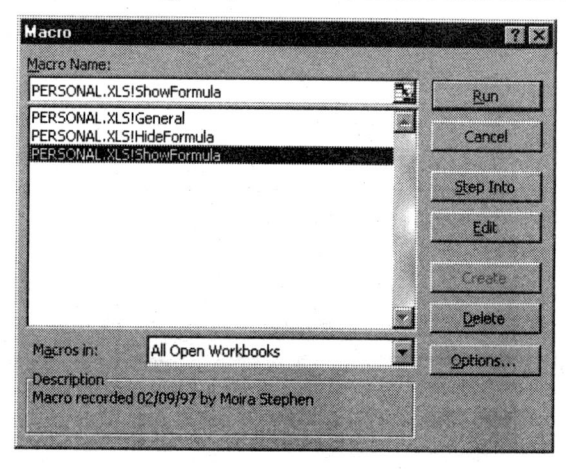

MACROS

9.5 Ideas for more macros

You can record almost anything you want into a macro. Some of the things that you could record into a macro may also be automated in other ways, e.g. AutoFormat or Styles. Macros are usually used to carry out a sequence of commands.

If you find that you regularly use a series of commands in the same order, or use an option that is buried deep in a dialog box, macros can help you speed up the way you work.

Try out the macros below to get some more practice. They are all easy to create.

Setting up a header and/or footer

If you use the same header and/or footer in many of your workbooks, you could record the command sequence into a macro.

1 Open the **Tools** menu, choose **Macro** then **Record New Macro...**

2 Give your macro a name – *HeaderFooter* or something similar

3 If you want a keyboard shortcut, click in the **Shortcut** field and enter the shortcut you want to use, e.g. *Ctrl+Shift+F*

4 Select the workbook to store the macro in – use the *Personal Macro Workbook* if you want it to available to all workbooks

5 Click **OK**

- You will be returned to your worksheet, and the **Stop Recording** toolbar will be displayed.

6 Open the **File** menu and choose **Page Setup...**

7 Select the **Header/Footer** tab

8 Set up the Header and/or Footer required

9 Click **OK**

10 Click the **Stop** tool on the **Stop Recording** toolbar when you've finished

Discount calculator

Let's say you offer a discount to your customers based on the amount of their order. You could record a simple discount calculator into a macro, then access the calculator from any workbook you were working in. This macro will:

- Create a new blank worksheet within your workbook.
- Enter the text and formula to the discount calculator.
- Protect the sheet so that only the *Amount of Order* details can be entered.

Try it out!

1 Create a new workbook, or open an existing workbook before you start recording your macro

2 Open the **Tools** menu, choose **Macro** then **Record New Macro...**

3 Give your macro a name – *DiscountCal* or something similar – and enter a keyboard shortcut if wanted

4 Select the workbook to store the macro in – use the *Personal Macro Workbook* if you want it to available to all workbooks

5 Click **OK**

- You will be returned to your worksheet.

6 Insert a new sheet – choose **Worksheet** from the **Insert** menu. Enter the text and formulas to calculate the *discount* (in this example, 7.5%) and *balance due* (see below – don't display the formulas)

	A	B
1	Total Amount of Order	
2		
3	Discount	=B1*7.5%
4		
5	Balance due	=B1-B3

MACROS

7 Unlock the cell that you will enter the *Amount of Order* into

8 Protect the worksheet (see Section 5.11)

9 Stop recording

If you recorded the macro in your Personal Macro Workbook, you can access it from anywhere using the keyboard shortcut, or run the macro from the Macro dialog box.

9.6 Deleting a macro

As you experiment with setting up macros, you will inevitably end up with some that you don't want to keep. They may not prove as useful as you first thought, or they might not run properly. You can easily delete any macro you no longer require.

If the macro you want to delete is in the Personal Macro Workbook, you must **Unhide** the workbook before you can edit it.

To unhide the Personal Macro Workbook:

1 Open the **Window** menu and choose **Unhide...**

2 Select the workbook – *Personal* in this case

3 Click **OK**

To delete a macro:

1 Open the **Tools** menu, select **Macro** then **Macros...**

3 Select the macro from the list displayed

4 Click **Delete**

5 Confirm the deletion at the prompt

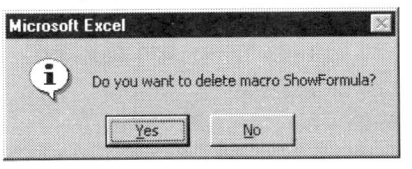

If you have displayed your Personal Macro Workbook, you must hide it again once you've deleted any macros you don't want to keep. *Do not* close it – if you do you won't be able to use the macros that you recorded in the workbook.

– 143 –

To hide the Personal Macro Workbook again:
- Open the **Window** menu and choose **Hide**.

If you accidentally close the Personal Macro Workbook, you can open it again using the Open command on the File menu.

If you have Microsoft Office installed on the C drive of your computer, your Personal Macro Workbook can be found in *C:\Program Files\Microsoft Office\Office\Xlstart*.

9.7 Editing a macro

I'd suggest you re-record any short macro that has an error in it rather than try to edit it – if it's a short macro you can probably re-record it as quickly as you could edit it.

However, if you have recorded a longer macro or have a minor adjustment to make to a macro, it's probably quicker to edit it rather than re-record the whole thing again.

The macros you record through the Macro Recorder are translated into Visual Basic – so things may look a bit strange when you first try editing a macro. But don't worry, if you take your time and have a look through the instructions you'll soon be able to relate your actions in Excel to the Visual Basic code.

When editing a macro, be very careful not to delete anything you don't understand, or insert anything that should not be there – you might find your macro no longer runs properly if you do.

If the worst comes to the worst and the macro stops working, you can always record it again.

When you look through the Visual Basic code there are often far more lines of code than commands you intentionally recorded through the Macro Recorder. Don't worry about this – some instructions are picked up from default settings in dialog boxes. Just scroll through until you see something you recognise as the line you want to change.

Let's try editing the discount amount in our discount calculator to make it 12.5%.

If the discount calculator macro is in the Personal Macro Workbook, you must unhide the workbook before you can edit the macro.

To unhide the Personal Macro Workbook:

1 Open the **Window** menu and choose **Unhide...**

2 Select the workbook – *Personal* in this case

3 Click **OK**

To edit the macro:

1 Open the **Tools** menu and choose **Macro** then **Macros...**

2 Select the macro you wish to edit

3 Click the **Edit** button

- The Visual Basic code for the selected macro will be displayed.

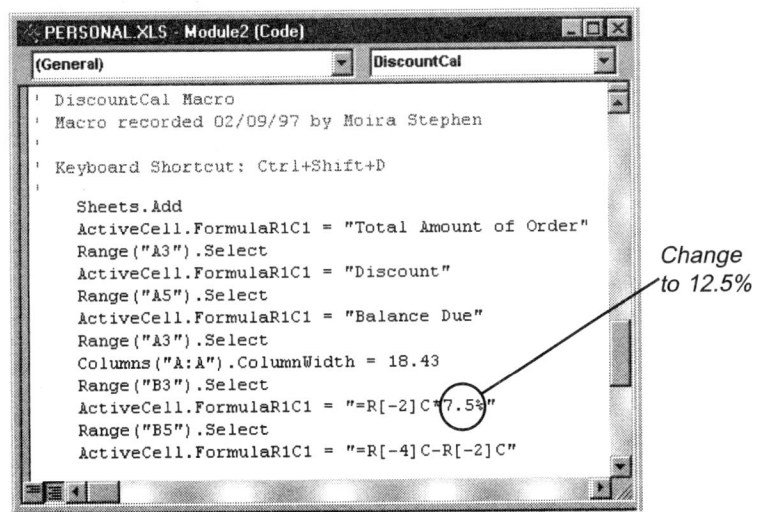

```
' DiscountCal Macro
' Macro recorded 02/09/97 by Moira Stephen
'
' Keyboard Shortcut: Ctrl+Shift+D
'
    Sheets.Add
    ActiveCell.FormulaR1C1 = "Total Amount of Order"
    Range("A3").Select
    ActiveCell.FormulaR1C1 = "Discount"
    Range("A5").Select
    ActiveCell.FormulaR1C1 = "Balance Due"
    Range("A3").Select
    Columns("A:A").ColumnWidth = 18.43
    Range("B3").Select
    ActiveCell.FormulaR1C1 = "=R[-2]C*7.5%"
    Range("B5").Select
    ActiveCell.FormulaR1C1 = "=R[-4]C-R[-2]C"
```

Change to 12.5%

4 Scroll through the code until you see the area you want to change

5 Edit as required

6 Save the changes – click the **Save** tool on the Standard toolbar
7 Close – click the **Close** button on the Microsoft Visual Basic title bar

9.8 Saving macros on exit

If you have saved some macros into your Personal Macro Workbook, a prompt will appear when you exit Excel, asking if you want to save the changes to that workbook.

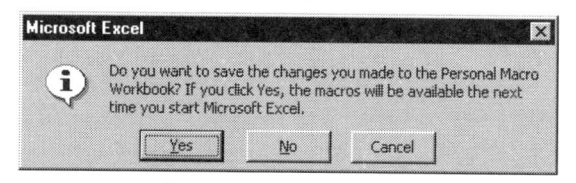

> **Microsoft Excel**
> Do you want to save the changes you made to the Personal Macro Workbook? If you click Yes, the macros will be available the next time you start Microsoft Excel.
> Yes   No   Cancel

If you want to be able to use the macros you have created the next time you use Excel, click **Yes** at the prompt.

9.9 Summary

In this chapter we have discussed macros. You have learnt how to:

- Record a macro using the Macro Recorder.
- Give the macro a keyboard shortcut.
- Run the macro.
- Delete a macro.
- Edit a macro using the Visual Basic Editor.
- Save the changes to the Personal Macro Workbook so that you can use them again the next time you use Excel.

10

TOOLBARS

10.1 Aims of this chapter

In this chapter we discuss toolbars. We'll look at basic toolbar manipulation – the positioning of toolbars on the screen and showing and hiding toolbars. We'll also discuss how you can edit existing toolbars, create new toolbars and assign macros to toolbars. Finally, we'll discuss some of the other options available when working with toolbars, including how to modify the image on a tool.

10.2 Moving toolbars

When working in Excel the Standard toolbar and Formatting toolbar are normally displayed along the top of your screen – the Standard one above the Formatting one.

Toolbars can be located in one of the four *docking* areas – at the top, bottom, left and right of the Excel window frame. You can also leave your toolbar *floating* anywhere on the screen if you prefer.

To move a toolbar:

If the toolbar is docked

1 Point to the left edge of the toolbar (if it is docked at the top or bottom of the screen) or top edge (if it is docked at the left or right of the screen) – where the two raised lines are

2 Drag and drop the toolbar into its new position

If the toolbar is not docked

1 Point to its Title Bar

2 Drag and drop the toolbar into its new position

10.3 Showing and hiding toolbars

You will have noticed that some toolbars appear and disappear automatically when you are working in Excel. You can also opt to show or hide toolbars whenever you wish. Provided you have at least one toolbar displayed, you can use the shortcut method to show or hide any toolbar.

To use the shortcut method:

1 Point to a toolbar

2 Click the *right* mouse button

- Any toolbars that are already displayed have a tick beside their name, any that are not displayed have no tick.

3 Click (using the *left* mouse button) on the toolbar name that you wish to show or hide

If no toolbars are displayed, you must use the View menu to show them again.

1 Open the **View** menu and choose **Toolbars**

2 Click on the one you want to show

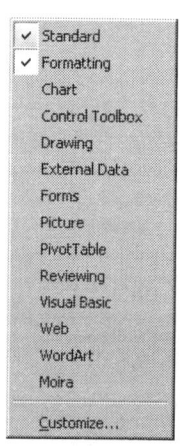

Using either of the methods above, you can show or hide one toolbar at a time. If you want to change the display status of several toolbars at the one time, it may be quicker to use the **Customize** dialog box.

1 Right click on a toolbar that is currently displayed

Or

- Open the **View** menu and choose **Toolbars**.

2 Click **Customize...**

3 Select or deselect the toolbars in the list as required (a tick means they are displayed, no tick means they are hidden)

4 Click **Close**

Turn off toolbars when you are not using them to give you a larger working area

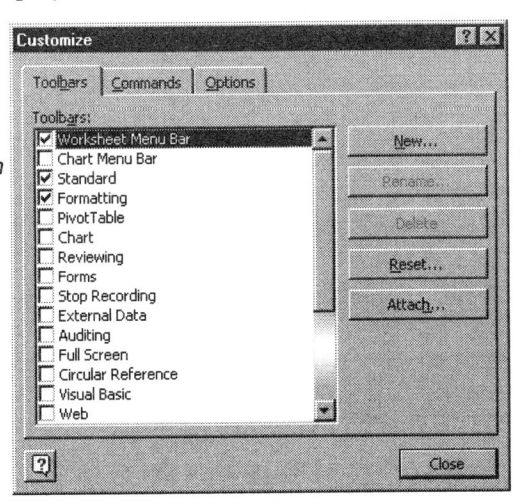

10.4 Editing existing toolbars

If you find that there are some tools on a toolbar that you tend not to use, or if you want to add another tool to a toolbar, you can edit the toolbar. If you want to add several tools to a toolbar, you should create a new toolbar and add your tools to it – see 10.5 below. If you want to edit a toolbar it must be displayed.

To edit an existing toolbar:

1 Display the toolbar you want to edit and right click on it

Or

- Open the **View** menu and choose **Toolbars**.

2 Click **Customize...**

3 Select the **Commands** tab

When the **Customize** dialog box is open, you can add tools to, move tools around on or remove tools from a toolbar.

To add a tool:

1 Select the **Category** of tool you're looking for

2 Locate the tool you require in the list

3 Drag it over to the toolbar – when you are over a toolbar a very dark I-beam with + beside it indicates your position – and drop it in the position required (if you are not over a toolbar, the mouse pointer has a small button with an x)

If you want a brief description of a tool's purpose, select it in the list of commands on the **Commands** tab, or on the toolbar, then click the **Description** button.

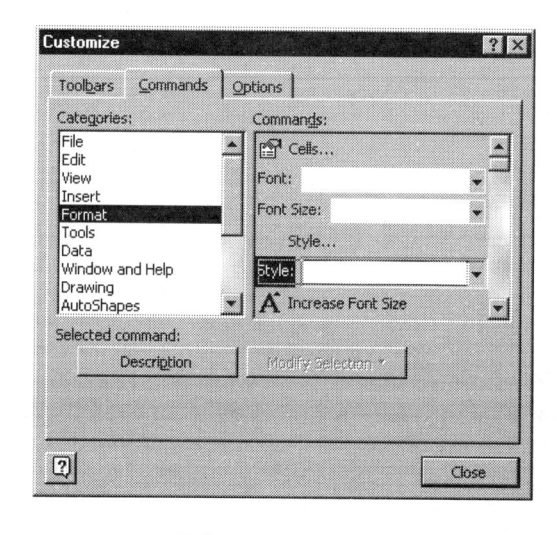

To move a tool:

1 Drag the tool to the correct position on the toolbar
2 Drop it

To remove a tool:

1 Drag the tool off the toolbar
2 Drop it anywhere

- Click **Close** in the **Customize** dialog box when you've finished editing your toolbar.

The drop-down lists that appear on toolbars, e.g. **Style** box and **Font** box on the Formatting toolbar, take up a lot more room than one of the smaller buttons.

If you need to free up some space on a toolbar that contains drop-down tools, you can change the size of these tools as required.

To change the size of a drop-down tool, you must have the **Customize** dialog box open.

1 On the appropriate toolbar, select the tool you want to resize, e.g. `Currency`

2 Click and drag the right or left edge of it – the mouse pointer becomes a thick double-headed arrow when you are in the correct place

---

SHORTCUT

You can quickly move or delete tools from a toolbar that is displayed without opening the Customize dialog box.

To move a tool: Hold down the **[Alt]** key and drag the tool along the toolbar (or to another toolbar)

To delete a tool: Hold down the **[Alt]** key and drag the tool off the toolbar

10.5 Creating a new toolbar

If you have several tools that you'd like to add to a toolbar (or macros that you want to assign to tools), you may find that you need to create a new toolbar, rather than try to squeeze tools into the existing toolbars.

To create a new toolbar:
1 Open the **Customize** dialog box
2 Select the **Toolbars** tab
3 Click **New...**
4 Give your toolbar a name and click **OK**

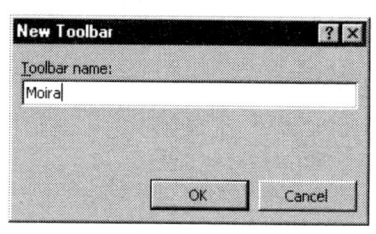

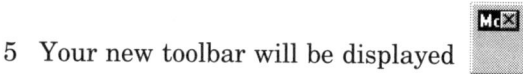

5 Your new toolbar will be displayed
6 Choose the **Commands** tab and add the tools you require to your new toolbar
7 **Close** the **Customize** dialog box

10.6 Adding macros to toolbars

In Chapter 9 we discussed macros. The macros you set up can be assigned to a tool on a toolbar, and run with a simple click!

To assign a macro to a toolbar:
1 Display the toolbar you want to assign your macro to
2 Open the **Customize** dialog box
3 Choose the **Commands** tab
4 Select the **Macros** category

5 Drag the **Custom Button** over onto your toolbar

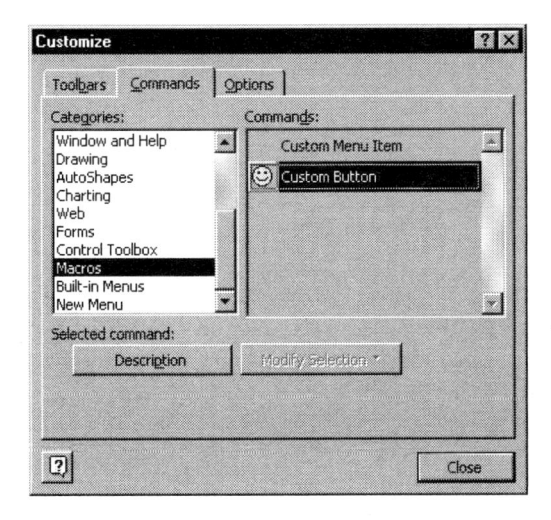

10.7 Change the button image

You may want to change the custom button image – things get a bit confusing if you use the same one for several macros! If you are assigning several macros to a toolbar, you don't want them all with a smiley face!

To change the button image:

1 Display the toolbar that has the macro button image on it
2 Open the **Customize** dialog box and select the **Commands** tab
3 Select the macro button on your toolbar
4 Click **Modify Selection**
5 Choose **Change Button Image**
6 Select an Image for your macro button

10.8 Assign a macro to a tool

To assign a macro to a tool on your toolbar:

1 Display the toolbar that has the macro button image on it
2 Open the **Customize** dialog box and select the **Commands** tab
3 Select the macro button on your toolbar
4 Click **Modify Selection**
5 Choose **Assign Macro...**
6 Select the macro you want to assign to the macro button
7 Click **OK**

The Screen Tip (see 1.9) that appears (should you choose to display them) when you point to a custom button is taken from the **Name** field in the **Modify Selection** list.

To display a message that reflects the purpose of the tool:

1 Display the toolbar that has the macro button image on it
2 Open the **Customize** dialog box and select the **Commands** tab
3 Select the macro button on your toolbar
4 Click **Modify Selection**
5 Select the text '*&Custom Button*' in the **Name:** field
6 Type in the text you want to display
7 Click anywhere off the list to close it
8 Close the **Customize** dialog box when you've finished

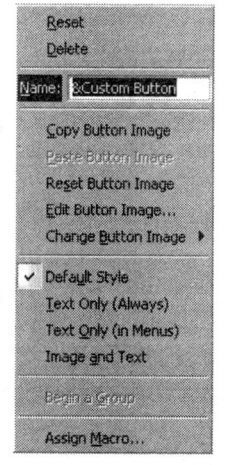

10.9 Resetting toolbars

If you have modified one of the preset toolbars that come with Excel, then decide you want to set it back to how it was when you installed the package, you can reset it to its original settings.

To reset an Excel toolbar:

1 Open the **Customize** dialog box
2 Select the **Toolbars** tab
3 Click on the toolbar you want to reset
4 Click the **Reset..** button

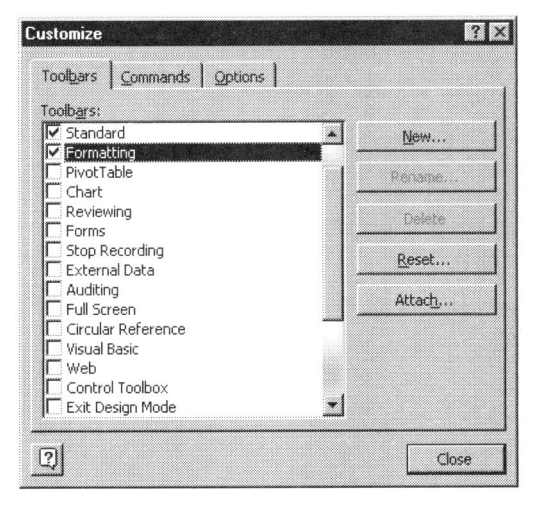

5 Respond to the prompt as appropriate – **OK** to reset the toolbar, **Cancel** if you've changed your mind

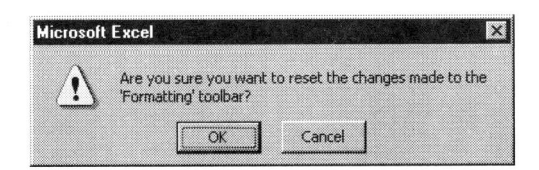

– 155 –

10.10 Summary

In this chapter we have considered the various options available when working with toolbars and when modifying toolbars. We have discussed:

- Positioning toolbars on your screen.
- Showing and hiding toolbars.
- Adding tools to toolbars.
- Moving tools on toolbars.
- Removing tools from toolbars.
- Creating new toolbars.
- Changing the custom button image.
- Assigning macros to a tool.
- Resetting an Excel toolbar.

11
EXCEL WITH OTHER APPLICATIONS

11.1 Aims of this chapter

Excel is part of the Microsoft Office suite, and it integrates very well with the other applications in the suite. If you have installed the complete suite then you have the benefit of being able to use the most appropriate tool for the job. This chapter discusses some of the ways in which Office applications can be integrated.

11.2 Linking vs embedding

Linking and embedding are techniques that enable you exchange data between Excel and other applications. The main differences between linked and embedded data lie in where it is stored and how it is updated.

LINKED DATA

Linked data *is not* stored in your Excel workbook. It is stored in a file – e.g. a document or presentation – in the source application (the application that it was created in). The data is updated within the source application – and those changes are reflected in the Excel workbook to which it is linked.

Advantages of linking data include:

- The workbook file is smaller than with embedded data.
- The data in the Excel workbook reflects the current status of the source data.

EMBEDDED DATA

Embedded data *is* stored in your Excel workbook. However, when you create and edit the data, you have access to all the functions within the source application.

Advantages of embedding data:

- All the data is held in one file.
- You have access to powerful functions that are not part of the Excel application when creating and editing the object.

The following sections discuss some of the methods you can use to integrate the data across the applications in Office.

11.3 Copy and Paste

You can copy text, data, graphics, charts, etc. from one application to another within the Office suite using simple copy and paste techniques. We will consider how you can copy charts and data *from* Excel into other applications in the Office suite.

To copy and paste:

1 Start Excel *and* the application you want to copy into

2 Open the workbook that you are copying from, and the file that will receive the copy

3 Select the chart or data you want to copy

4 Click the **Copy** tool on the Standard toolbar

5 Switch to the application you want to copy into

6 Place the insertion point where you want the chart or data to appear

7 Click the **Paste** tool on the Standard toolbar

When you copy charts and data in this way, the chart or data is not 'linked' to the original data in the Excel workbook in any way. Should you edit the data in Excel, the data you copied into the destination file remains as it was when you copied it.

You can copy and paste data and charts from Excel into a Word document or a PowerPoint presentation using this technique.

11.4 Copy and Paste Special

If you want the data that you copy into your file to be kept in line with the data held in Excel, you should create a link to it. You must use copy and paste special to create a link.

To copy and paste special:

1 Start Excel and the application you want to copy data into

2 Select the chart or data you want to copy

3 Click the **Copy** tool on the Standard toolbar

4 Switch to the application you want to copy into

5 Place the insertion point where you want the chart or data to appear

6 Open the **Edit** menu and choose **Paste Special**

7 Select the **Paste Link** button

8 Choose an option from the **As:** list – when you select an option a brief description of how it works appears in the **Result** box

9 Click **OK**

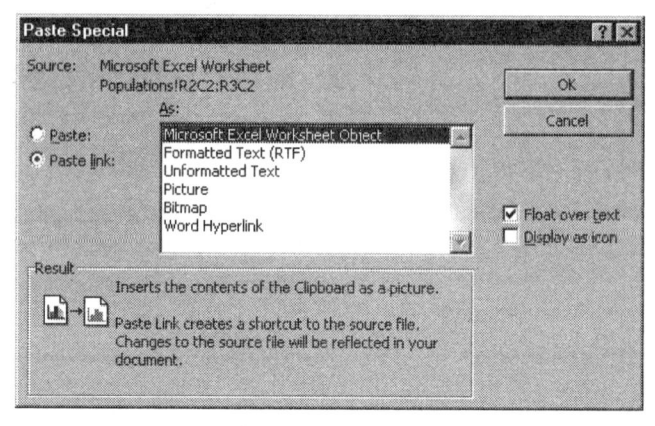

When you copy charts and data in this way, the chart or data displayed in the destination file is linked to the original data in Excel. Should you edit the data in Excel, the data in your Word document or PowerPoint presentation will be updated automatically.

11.5 Insert Excel Worksheet

You can obviously copy and paste, or paste special to get data or charts from Excel into a Word or PowerPoint file. However, if you want data in Word or PowerPoint, and it isn't already set up in Excel (and doesn't need to be), you can insert an Excel worksheet into a Word or PowerPoint file. The worksheet you insert will be created and edited using Excel functions.

The Excel worksheet you insert will be an embedded object.

To insert a Microsoft Excel Worksheet:

1 Place the insertion point where you want the worksheet to appear in your Word document or PowerPoint presentation

2 Click the **Insert Microsoft Excel Worksheet** tool on the Standard toolbar

EXCEL WITH OTHER APPLICATIONS

3 Click and drag over the grid to specify the worksheet size

- You end up with an embedded worksheet, with the toolbars and menus of Excel displayed.

4 Set up your worksheet as normal

5 Click anywhere outside the worksheet area to return to your Word document or PowerPoint presentation

- To edit your worksheet, double click on it – you will be returned to Excel.

11.7 Microsoft Map

Pictures often talk louder than words, and this is particularly true if you are presenting figures and want to show trends or patterns. In Chapter 6 we discussed using charts to display the data in your worksheet. In this section, we will see how you can use maps to display your data.

If you record *geographic* statistical data in an Excel worksheet, you can use Microsoft Map to display the data graphically.

If you did not select this feature when you installed Excel, you will need to re-run Setup to install this before going any further.

To install Microsoft Map:

1 Close all applications that are currently running

2 Click **Start**, choose **Settings**, then **Control Panel**

3 Double click the **Add/Remove Programs** icon

4 Choose *Microsoft Office 97* from the list

5 Click **Add/Remove**

6 Insert your Microsoft Office CD at the prompt and click **OK**

7 Click **Add/Remove**

– 161 –

8 Select *Microsoft Excel*

9 Click **Change Option...**

10 Select *Microsoft Map* and click **OK**

11 Follow the prompts until you have Microsoft Map installed

Worked Example

In this example, we have recorded the populations of some European countries in our worksheet.

We now want to display this data on a map of Europe.

For a list of standard spellings and abbreviations for map features, see *Mapstats.xls* in the Data folder. The exact location of this folder depends on where Microsoft Map is installed, but try *C:\Program Files\Common Files\Microsoft Shared\Datamap\Data*.

	A	B	C
1	Country	Population	
2	Austria	7,620,000	
3	Belgium	9,920,000	
4	Denmark	5,140,000	
5	France	56,200,000	
6	Germany	79,100,000	
7	Greece	10,100,000	
8	Italy	57,600,000	
9	Ireland	3,574,000	
10	Netherlands	14,900,000	
11	Norway	4,230,000	
12	Poland	37,900,000	
13	Portugal	10,300,000	
14	Spain	39,500,000	
15	Switzerland	6,670,000	
16	Sweden	8,530,000	
17	UK	57,200,000	
18			

To create the map:

1 Select the data you wish to display, including column headings

2 Click the **Map** tool on the Standard toolbar

3 Click and drag on a blank area of your worksheet to indicate the position and size of your map

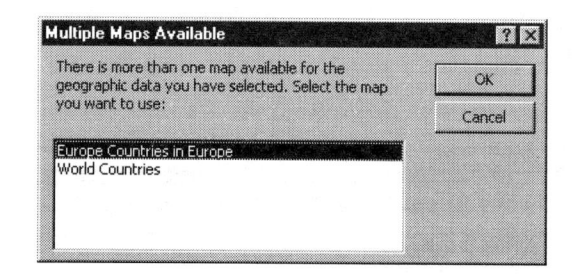

4 If the **Multiple Maps Available** dialog box appears, select the map you wish to use and click **OK**

- Your map will appear on your worksheet, together with the **Microsoft Map Control** dialog box.

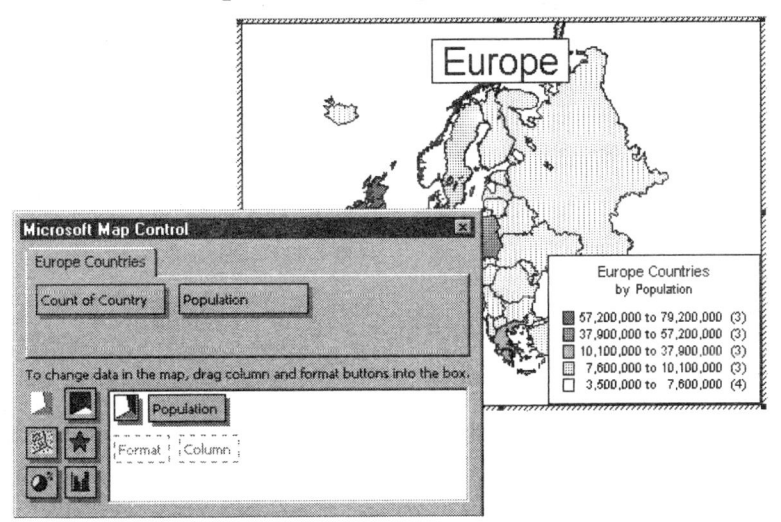

- For the time being, let's assume that you're happy with the map the way it is. Click anywhere outside the map area to return to the sheet.

Move, resize and delete the map

You can move, resize or delete the map that you have embedded within your worksheet in the same way as you can a chart. The map must be selected *before* you can move, resize or delete it.

- To select a map in your worksheet, click on it once.

To move the map:

1 Drag the map to its new position

To resize the map:

1 Point to one of the handles along the edge of the map area

2 Drag the handle to increase or decrease the size of the object

To delete the map:

1 Press the **[Delete]** key on your keyboard

If you wish to make any other changes to your map, you must use the functions available within Microsoft Map.

- You can return your map to the Microsoft Map environment by double clicking on it.

When working in Microsoft Map, the Microsoft Map toolbar is displayed. You can use this to modify or enhance your map in a number of ways.

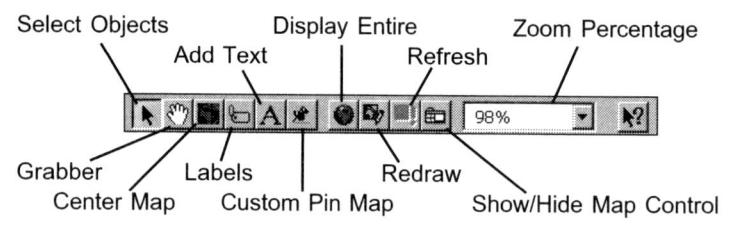

Select Objects — Display Entire — Zoom Percentage
Add Text — Refresh

Grabber — Labels — Redraw
Center Map — Custom Pin Map — Show/Hide Map Control

The best way to see how the various tools on the toolbar work is to experiment with them.

SELECT OBJECTS

You can select individual objects within your map using this tool – the two objects displayed in this example are the map title and the map key.

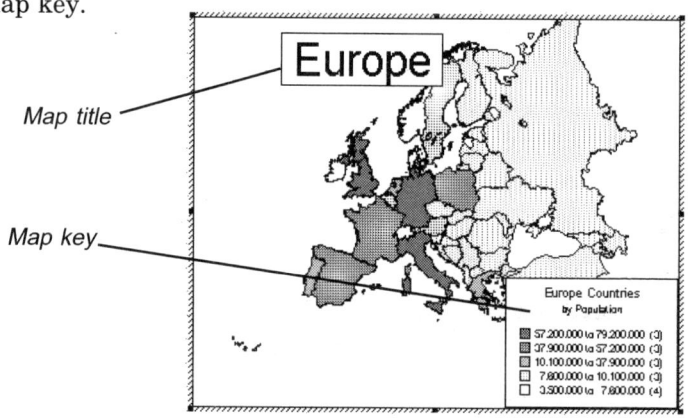

Map title — Europe

Map key

To select an object:

1 Click on the **Select Objects** tool if required

2 Click on the object to be selected

When an object is selected you can move, resize or delete it using the same techniques as when moving, resizing and deleting a map or chart within a worksheet.

- If you delete an object, then want to display it again, open the View menu and select the object you wish to display – Title, Subtitle or All Legends – from there.

You can edit the text, or format the font, in the map title or subtitle.

To edit the text:

1 Double click on the object

2 Edit the text as required

3 Click outside the object when you're finished

To format the font:

1 *Right* click on the object

2 Choose **Format Font...**

3 Select the formatting options required and click **OK**

To modify the key:

1 Double click on the object

2 Make the changes required in the **Format** dialog box

3 Click **OK**

GRABBER

This tool lets you move the map within its designated area.

To move the map:

1 Select the **Grabber** tool

2 Drag the map right, left, up or down as required

3 Click the **Grabber** tool again, or select a different tool

Center Map

You can centre your map on a specific point using this tool.

1 Select the **Center Map** tool

2 Click on the area of your map you want the map centred on

3 Click the **Center Map** tool again, or select a different tool

Map Labels

You can use these to display a label showing either the country name or another feature. The labels will display when you move your mouse pointer over the appropriate area on your map.

To select a map label:

1 Click the **Map Labels** tool

2 Select the option you want in the **Map Labels** dialog box

3 Click **OK**

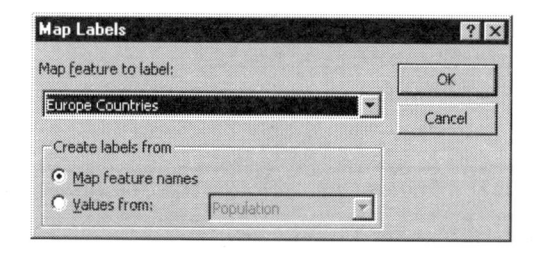

Add Text

Each map can have a Title and Subtitle object to describe the map that is displayed. If you wish to add more text to your map, you can do so using the Add Text tool.

1 Select the **Add Text** tool

2 Click where you want to enter the text on your map

3 Type in the text

4 Repeat steps 2 and 3 until you've added all the text required

5 Click the **Add Text** tool again, or select another tool

Custom Pin Map

You can add your own labels (or pins) to your maps if you wish.

1 Select the **Custom Pin Map** tool
2 If the **Custom Pin Map** dialog box appears, enter a name for your map in the dialog box or select an existing map
3 Click **OK**
4 On your map, click at each place you want to add a 'pin'
5 Click the **Custom Pin Map** again, or select another tool

- If you add a pin, then change your mind, select it (click on it) and press the [**Delete**] key on your keyboard.

Display Entire

Centres the map and zooms out to show it all

Redraw Map

Minimises the 'stretching' effect on your map, if you have moved it using the Grabber.

Map Refresh

If you change the data on which the map is based, this tool becomes activated. Click it to update your map.

Show/Hide Microsoft Map Control

Toggles the display of the Microsoft Map Control box (illustrated on page 163).

Zoom Percentage of Map

Use this tool to change the zoom percentage of your map. Either click the drop-down arrow and choose a percentage from the list, or click in the box and type in the percentage zoom you want.

- Explore the menus and on-line Help system within Microsoft Map to see what other features are available.

11.8 Summary

In this chapter we have discussed some of the ways you can integrate Excel with the rest of the Microsoft Office suite. We have discussed:

- Copy and Paste.
- Linking the source data in an Excel workbook with the copy in Word or PowerPoint using Copy and Paste Special.
- Embedding an Excel worksheet in Word and PowerPoint.
- Using Microsoft Map to display geographical statistics.

12
EXCEL AND THE WEB

12.1 Aims of this chapter

This chapter discusses using Excel with the wider world. You will learn how to e-mail an Excel workbook. You will also learn how to use hyperlinks to link to other files on your own computer or network, and to pages on the World Wide Web (affectionately called the Web). Finally, we'll create a Web page from within Excel and discuss how to publish it to the Web. The examples are based on the use of Microsoft Outlook for e-mail. You must also have access to the Internet for this chapter.

12.2 E-mail

Provided you have a modem, communications software and a service provider, you can e-mail your Excel workbook to anywhere in the world. When you e-mail a workbook, you send it electronically over a computer network. E-mail is usually very fast – sometimes your message will be delivered almost instantly, other times it may take longer.

If you use Microsoft Word as well as Excel, specify Word as your e-mail editor in Outlook. You can then format your text, create tables, bulleted lists, etc. using familiar Word features.

To specify Word as your e-mail editor:

1 Start **Outlook** – click the **Start** button on the Taskbar, choose **Programs** then select **Microsoft Outlook**

2 Open the **Tools** menu and choose **Options...**

3 Select **Use Word as the e-mail editor** on the **E-mail** tab

4 Click **OK**

Another useful option is the automatic saving of sent messages.

To check the status of this option on your machine:

1 Open the **Tools** menu in **Outlook**

2 Choose **Options...**

3 Select the **Sending** tab

- If the **Save copies of messages in Sent Items folder** checkbox is selected, a copy of everything you send will be saved automatically in the *Sent Items* folder. The folder is displayed in the *Mail* category on the Outlook Bar.

4 Select or de-select this option as required

If you are not familiar with Outlook, explore it now. You'll find lots of useful features that will try to make you more efficient!

Provided you have a workbook open in Excel, you can e-mail that workbook directly from Excel. The workbook you have open in Excel will become an 'attachment' to your mail message.

To e-mail a workbook from within Excel:

1 Open the workbook you want to e-mail

2 Choose **Send To** from the **File** menu

3 Select **Mail Recipient...**

- If Outlook is not running, the **Choose Profile** dialog box will appear as the application opens. Select your profile name from the dialog box and click **OK.**

4 Enter the e-mail address you want to send the message to (or click the **To...** button and select the address from the list)

5 Enter or edit the **Subject** as necessary

6 Type in your message

- The current workbook is an attachment to your mail message.

7 Click **Send**

8 Close your message

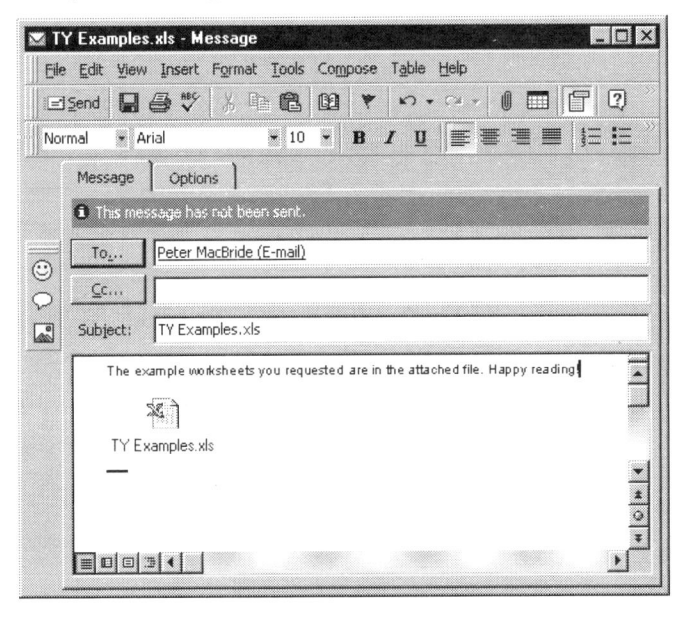

To attach a workbook from within Outlook:

1 Select **Inbox** on the Outlook Bar (down the left of the screen)

2 Click the **New Mail Message** tool

3 Enter the address in the **To:** field and **Cc:** field if necessary

4 Type in your **Subject**

5 Key in your message

To attach a file:

6 Click the **Insert File** tool

7 Select the file you want to attach

8 Click **OK**

9 Repeat 6-8 if you want to attach more than one file

10 Send your message

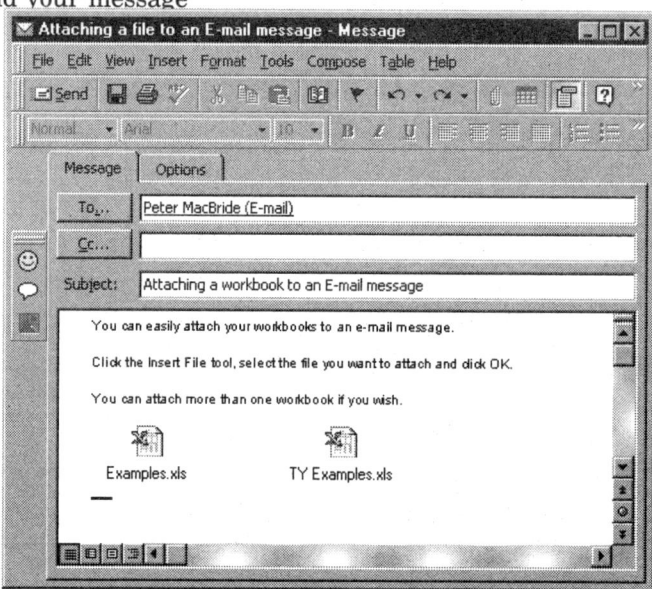

To read an e-mail you receive:

1 Click **Inbox** in the Outlook Bar

2 Double click on the message you want to read

3 If the message has files attached to it, double click the attachment icon to read the file

You can use the tools on the Outlook toolbar to reply, reply to all, forward, print and delete your e-mail messages.

EXCEL AND THE WEB

12.3 Hyperlinks

A hyperlink is a 'hot spot' that lets you jump from your workbook to another location – on your own computer, on your company network or anywhere in the world via the Internet.

- The Internet is a collection of thousands of computers and computer networks that are scattered throughout the world. You can access the data on these computers if you are connected to the Internet.

You can insert a hyperlink anywhere in your workbook. When you click one, the file that it points to is displayed on your screen.

To insert a hyperlink to a file:

1 Select the cell you want to place your hyperlink in

2 Click the **Insert Hyperlink** tool on the Standard toolbar

3 Type in the path and name of the file you want to jump to

Or

- Click **Browse...** and locate the file on your system using the **Link to File** dialog box.

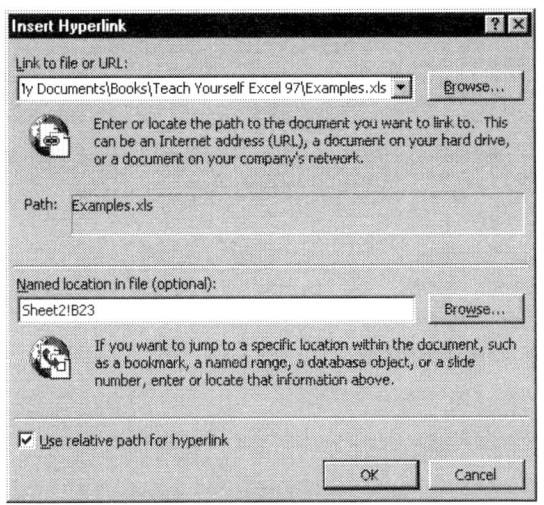

Browse to find your file...

... and perhaps browse again to locate a named place

4 If you have a named location in your file, e.g. a sheet name or named range in a workbook or a bookmark in a document, complete the **Named location in file** field if you want to jump to that point.

- Click the **Browse** button to open the dialog box to help you specify the location required. Enter a cell reference and choose the Sheet name required, or select the **Defined name** option and choose the named range you wish to jump to. Click **OK**

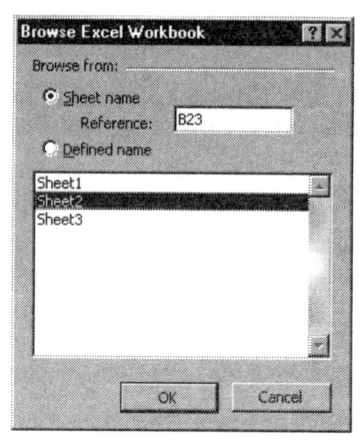

5 Click **OK** at the **Insert Hyperlink** dialog box.

The hyperlink will be inserted into your workbook. The text usually appears blue, with a blue underline. The hyperlink Examples.xls – Sheet2!B23 jumps to a cell B23 on Sheet 2 in an Excel workbook called Examples.

To insert a hyperlink to a URL on the Web:

1 Select the cell you want to place your hyperlink in

2 Click the **Insert Hyperlink** tool on the Standard toolbar

3 Type in the URL (Universal Resource Locator – the Internet address) of the file you want to jump to

Or

- Click **Browse...** so that you can search the Web

- If you opt to Browse, click the **Search the Web** tool in the **Link to File** dialog box

4 Locate the page you want to link to

5 Return to Excel – click **Microsoft Excel** on the Task Bar

6 Click **OK** at the **Insert Hyperlink** dialog box

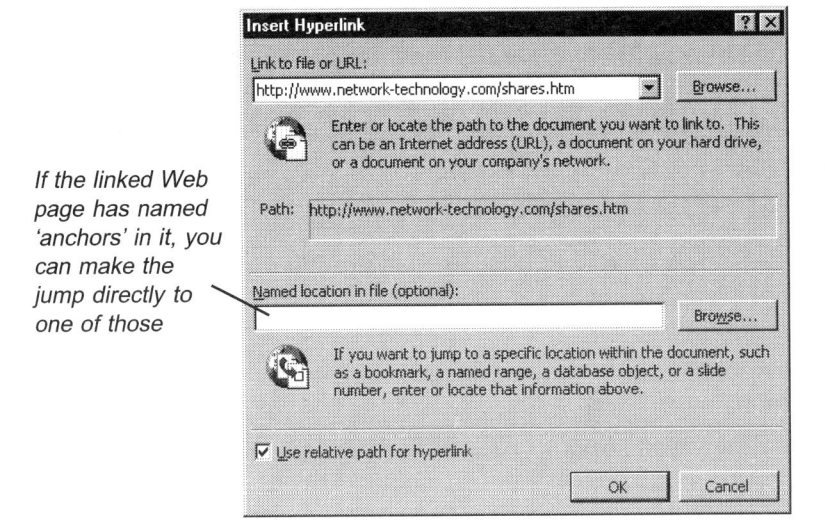

EXCEL AND THE WEB

If the linked Web page has named 'anchors' in it, you can make the jump directly to one of those

Let's get user-friendly!

In the examples above, the path or URL of the file or page the hyperlink points to is displayed in a cell in your workbook. You may prefer to display a more user-friendly prompt in place of the path or address. The prompt is an alternative display to the normal URL or path and file name – the URL or path and file name is hidden behind the prompt.

1 Type the text for your hyperlink prompt into a cell in your workbook, e.g. 'Network Technology Share Prices'

2 Select the cell that contains the text

3 Click the **Insert Hyperlink** tool on the Standard toolbar

4 Enter the path or URL (or Browse until you locate what you want)

5 Click **OK** at the **Insert Hyperlink** dialog box

The hyperlink has been inserted into your workbook, displaying the prompt – 'Network Technology Share Prices' – rather than the path or address that it actually points to.

To jump to a hyperlink location:

1 Point to the hyperlink – the mouse pointer becomes a hand with a pointing finger – and click

When you jump to a hyperlink location, the **Web** toolbar is displayed.

If the toolbar doesn't appear, click the **Web toolbar** tool on the Standard toolbar to display it. This tool toggles the display of the toolbar.

To return to the workbook, click the **Back** tool on the Web toolbar.

Once you've jumped to a hyperlink, then returned to your workbook, the hyperlink field changes colour – usually to violet. This will remind you that you've already used that hyperlink.

To remove a hyperlink:

1. Select the cell that contains the hyperlink in your worksheet
2. Press **[Delete]**

12.4 Preparing a Web page

The pages you access through the Internet are part of the World Wide Web. You can create your own pages from Excel and publish them on the Web if you wish.

To prepare a page for the Web you must save your data in an HTML file.

To save a range of cells or a chart in HTML format:

1. Open the workbook you want to prepare for publication
2. Select the range of cells and/or chart you want to save in HTML format
3. Choose **Save As HTML...** from the **File** menu

- The Office Assistant appears – he'll step you through the process if you ask him!
4. Work through the 4 steps of the Wizard selecting the options you require (if you're in any doubt about what to choose, stick to the defaults as they are usually fine)

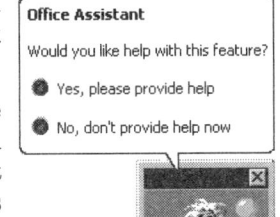

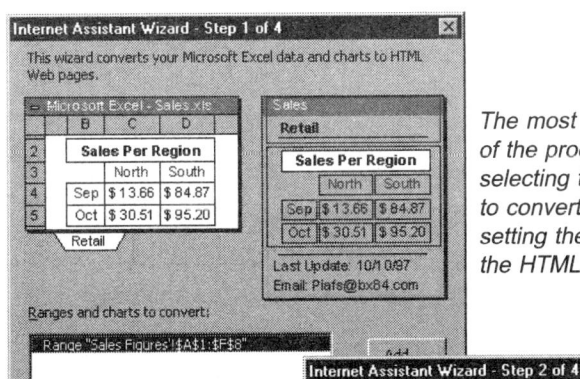

The most important parts of the process are selecting the range of data to convert (left), and setting the basic nature of the HTML page

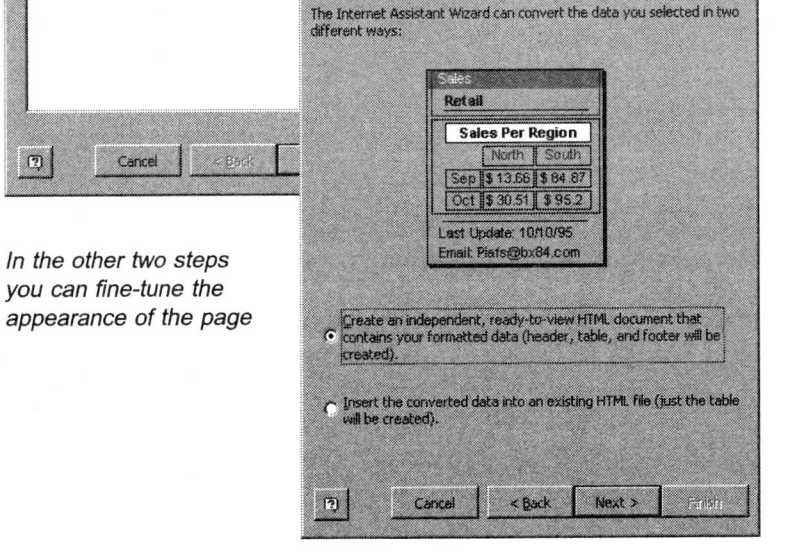

In the other two steps you can fine-tune the appearance of the page

12.5 Previewing your Web page

Once you've created your page, you should preview it before you publish. You must use your Web browser to see how your file will look as a Web page.

To preview your Web page:
1 Start up your Web browser
2 In your browser, choose **Open** from the **File** menu (if you're using Microsoft Internet Explorer) or **Open File** from the **File** menu (if you're using Netscape Navigator)
3 Locate and select the HTML file you want to view
4 Open the file

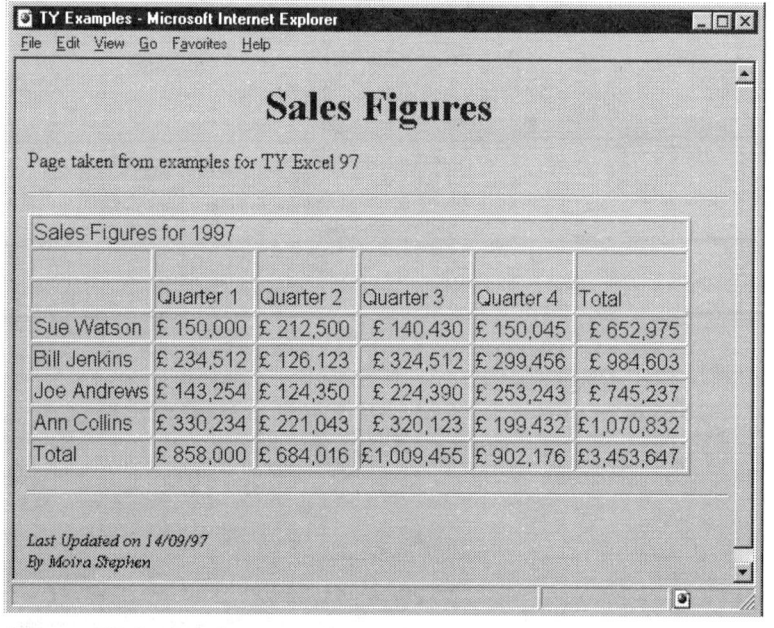

Sales Figures

Page taken from examples for TY Excel 97

Sales Figures for 1997					
	Quarter 1	Quarter 2	Quarter 3	Quarter 4	Total
Sue Watson	£ 150,000	£ 212,500	£ 140,430	£ 150,045	£ 652,975
Bill Jenkins	£ 234,512	£ 126,123	£ 324,512	£ 299,456	£ 984,603
Joe Andrews	£ 143,254	£ 124,350	£ 224,390	£ 253,243	£ 745,237
Ann Collins	£ 330,234	£ 221,043	£ 320,123	£ 199,432	£1,070,832
Total	£ 858,000	£ 684,016	£1,009,455	£ 902,176	£3,453,647

Last Updated on 14/09/97
By Moira Stephen

If your file looks okay, you're ready to go ahead and publish it. If you're not satisfied with it, go back into Excel and try again.

12.6 Publishing to the Web

To publish your HTML file to the Web you must copy your file from your own computer to your service provider's server. Your service provider's server will be switched on 24 hours a day, so anyone who knows the URL of your Web page will be able to access it at any time.

Most service providers will allocate some free storage space to you for your own Web pages – 10 Mb (about 7 diskettes' worth) is fairly typical.

There are a number of ways to upload files to a service provider's server – contact your service provider to find out how to upload your files to their server.

If you have created hyperlinks in your Web page that jump to other files on your computer, remember to upload *all* the files, not just the main page.

12.7 Summary

This final chapter has suggested ways of interacting with the wider world from Excel. We have covered:

- Send and receive e-mail messages.
- Create hyperlinks to other files.
- Create hyperlinks to Web pages.
- Display a user-friendly prompt for hyperlinks.
- Create pages for publication to the Web.
- Find out how to publish your Web pages.

INDEX

A

Advanced Filter 130
Alignment
  Across cells 48
  Within cells 47
Arrow 109
AutoFill 34
AutoFilter 128
AutoFormat 114
AutoShapes 110
AutoSum 70

B

Background colour of cells 50
Bold 46
Borders 50
Bring Forward 112

C

Callouts 110
Cell 17
  Addresses 79
  Borders 97
  Moving/copying contents 37
  Protection 97
  Range 21
Chart
  Create without Chart
    Wizard 106
  Default 108
  Formatting 104
  Print 107
  Separate sheet 106
Chart objects 104
Chart Wizard 100
Circular references 82, 127
Close 40
Columns 17, 26
  Headings 60
  Width 26
Comments 95
Copy and Paste
  Between applications 158
  Paste Special 159

D

Data form 135
Data validation 133
Database
  Records 123
  Field 123
  Field names 123
Default font 49
  Change 53
Drawing tools 108

E

E-mail 169, 170
Embedded data 158
Excel screen 6
Exiting Excel 16

F

Field 123
Flip 112
Font 49
Font colour 49
Font size 49
Footers 59, 141
Format painter 52
Formatting 46
Formulas 19, 31, 84
  Natural language 84

Formula Palette 73
Freeze panes 54
Functions 19

G
Gridlines 60
Grouping objects 111
Grouping worksheets 68

H
Hardware requirements 2
Headers 59, 141
Help
  Contents Tab 12
  Dialog Box 15
  Find Tab 14
  Index Tab 13
  Office Assistant 9
  Screentips 14
  What's This? 11
Hyperlink 173
  Delete 176
  Insert 173
  Jump to 176

I
IF function 90
Insert Excel Worksheet 160
Installing Excel 3
Internet 173
Internet Assistant Wizard 176
Italic 46

K
Keyboard shortcuts
Formatting 47
Macros 139
Menus 8

L
Line 109

Linked data 157

M
Macro 137
  Delete 143
  Edit 144, 145
  Play back 140
  Saving 146
Macro recorder 138
Margins 57
Menus
  Using the keyboard 8
  Using the mouse 8
Merge and Center 48
Microsoft Map 161

N
Natural language formulas 84
New 44

O
Office Assistant 9
  Customise 10
  Tips 11
Open 44
Operators 32
  Order of precedence 33
Orientation 56
Outlook 169
Oval 109

P
Page breaks 58
Page layout 56
Page order 61
Page size 57
Parentheses 33
Paste Special 159
Personal Macro Workbook
  Hide 144
  Open 144
  Unhide 143

Print 42
   Gridlines 60
   Preview 42
   Row & Column headings 60

R

Record 123
Rectangle 109
Rotate 112
Rows 17
   Headings 60

S

Save 39
   As 41
Scaling 57
Selection techniques 21
Send Backward 112
Software requirements 2
Sort 124
   Columns 126
   Multi-level 125
Split screen 55
Starting Excel
   Shortcut bar 5
   Start menu 5
Startup folder 120
Statistical functions 74
Styles 115
   Apply 116
   Create new 117
   Delete 117
   Edit 116
   Merge 117

T

Tab split box 63
Template 118
   Workbook 118
   Worksheet 120
Text
   Editing 24
   Wrap 28
Text boxes 110
Tool
   Assign Macro 154
Toolbar
   Assign Macro 152
   Chart 103
   Edit 149
   Modify button 153
   Move 147
   New 152
   Outlook 172
   Reset 154
   Shortcut Bar 5
   Show/hide 148
   Web 176

U

Underline 46
URL 174

W

Web Page
   Preparing 176
   Preview 178
   Publish 179
What's This? 11
Workbook
   Templates 118
Workbooks 7
Worksheet 7
   Add 64
   Copy 67
   Delete 66
   Design 63
   Group 68
   Move 67
   Moving between 62
   Rename 67